IRON CLIPPER

- 'Tayleur

the White Star Line's

'First Titanic'

H.F STARKEY

avid publications

Cover Illustrations:
Front: Artists' impression of *Tayleur* under tow down the River Mersey.
Rear:'The Last of England' by Ford Madox Brown. (Birmingham City Art Gallery)
Frontispiece: **The 'First Titanic' - the White Star's Iron Clipper** *Tayleur.*
This lithograph was drawn even before *Tayleur* had been fitted with her rigging.
The artist, O.P.Williams, imagines the ship as she would appear under full sail.

Further copies of this book are available from:-
Avid Publications
Garth Boulevard,
Bebington, Wirral,
Merseyside. U.K.
CH63 5LS
Tel / Fax (44) 0151 645 2047
e-mail: info@AvidPublications.co.uk

Other publications from Avid are detailed at the rear of this book.

Iron Clipper - *'Tayleur'*, The White Star Line's First Titanic.
ISBN 1 902964 00 4
© H.F.Starkey 1999

IRON CLIPPER
'Tayleur'-the White Star Line's 'First Titanic'
by

H.F. STARKEY

Contents

Preface

It was while researching nineteenth century river transport and its effects upon the economic development of mid-Merseyside that my attention was drawn to reports of the construction in Warrington of the largest merchant sailing ship of her time. I dismissed the stories of the great vessel as being absurd. I reasoned that if the largest Mersey sailing flats operating to Warrington displaced a mere eighty tons, it would be an impossibility for a ship of two thousand tons to be launched from Bank Quay. How could such a vessel make her way down this shallow, serpentine upper river to deep water at the estuary? The idea was too fantastic to be true. However, when I looked into archives and old newspapers I discovered that indeed, a huge iron clipper ship had been built in Warrington for the Australian trade. She was lost in the Irish Sea in January 1854 on her maiden voayge with the loss of nearly three hundred passengers and crew.

This is the story of the first White Star liner to be lost on her maiden voyage, the '*Tayleur*'.

I am pleased to acknowledge the help afforded me by Mr. Frank Corr of Dublin; Mr. Tom MacGinty of the Maritime Institute of Ireland, Dun Laoghaire, Ireland; Mr. D.V. Craig of the Public Record Office of Ireland, Dublin; Miss J.E. Hayes and Mr. Peter Rogerson of the Warrington Museum and Art Galleries and the late Peter Norton of Warrington. I wish to also acknowledge the help given to me by Veronica Oldham who was most generous in supplying me with details from her own research.

I am also indebted to Mrs. Carol Verey who typed the manuscript and to Mr. Gerry Starkey for art work.

To Pat and Gerard

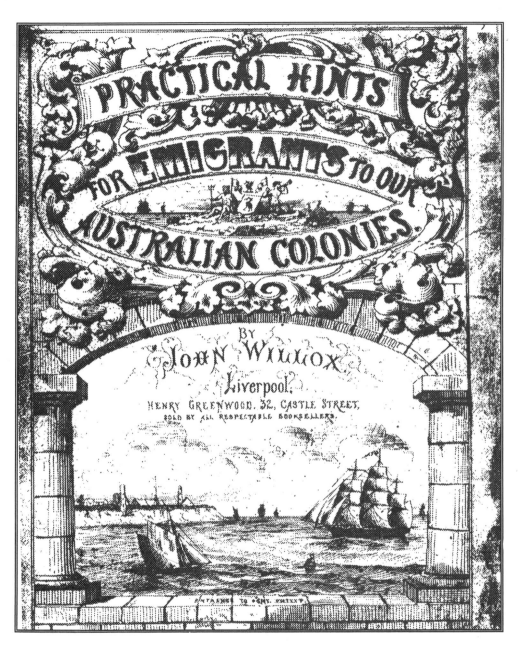

PRACTICAL HINTS

FOR EMIGRANTS TO OUR AUSTRALIAN COLONIES.

BY
JOHN WILLOX

Liverpool.

HENRY GREENWOOD, 52, CASTLE STREET,
SOLD BY ALL RESPECTABLE BOOKSELLERS.

A pamphlet of hints for the emigrant, written and printed in Liverpool.
Containing advice on everything from choosing a port of embarkation
(Liverpool is highly recommended), to selecting the necessary outfit and coping
with life on the voyage.

In 1854 the loss of the White Star Liner *'Tayleur'* on her maiden voyage with the deaths of hundreds of her passengers was to foreshadow another White Star disaster half a century later.

It has always been accepted that history repeats itself but the coincidences in the tragedy of the *'Tayleur'* and that of the *'Titanic'* stretch the imagination to incredulity.

SUPPLEMENT TO THE WARRINGTON GAZETTE.

AN ACCOUNT OF THE

FEARFUL WRECK OF THE TAYLEUR,

On LAMBAY ISLAND, JANUARY 21st, 1854.

In the long list of accidents and vicissitudes with which humanity has to contend, none seem so entirely uncontrollable and so terrible in their detail, as those constantly recurring on the deep. Knowledge and experience, united to genius and capacity, has, it is true, done much to improve the science of navigation, and tempted the aspiring spirit of men to extend his discoveries to the most remote corners of the globe; but still the sea is the sea, and against its mighty anger nothing earthly can contend:—

"Who shall appease thee; who, but One, shall say—
'Thus far thou shalt, but yet no farther stray!'
For though Canute himself were on the strand,
Thou wouldst not heed his majesty's command."

Now placid and calm—smiling back, as it were, the rays of sunshine from its dancing surface—in one short hour it may be rolling and surging with anger. Woe then to the ship tossed upon its bosom! for the strongest vessel built by man can no more stand against its power than a frail reed before a mighty wind.

Of all the disasters by sea, recorded during a season unhappily distinguished by such calamities, not one has been an-

seen, and little thought they who then beheld the fine ship—

"Like a thing of life,"

sweep so gallantly down the river,—cheering her on her way, and admiring her splendid contour—how soon she would lie a useless wreck beneath the wave! Little thought those emigrants, who from various causes had resolved to leave their country—some perhaps to meet dear friends in the distant colony, some in the pursuit of wealth, but no doubt most generally poor industrious sons of toil, who hoped in the far-off land to better their condition—little thought they how short would be their earthly voyage, and how brief their passage to eternity, how, in

"That bourne from which no traveller returns,"

their hopes, and fears, and speculations would be so shortly buried.

In disasters of this kind, the actual witnesses of the scene may naturally be supposed to furnish the most accurate account of the circumstances, and for this reason, we have deemed it better to preserve the statements in the language of those relators who were present.

The *Tayleur* left Liverpool, bound for Melbourne, on

From the statement of Captain Noble we are given to understand that the ship would not answer her helm, and that she was unmanageable in rough weather. As a refutation of this, however, we have the following statement of the pilot who took the *Tayleur* out to sea.

"I took the *Tayleur* to sea on Thursday, January 21st, the ship being in tow of the steamer *Victory*. While the wind was light the steamer continued towing her, but as soon as a breeze sprung up, the steamer was obliged to drop astern, as such were the sailing qualities of the ship that she would have run over the steamer. During the passage down I had full opportunity to examine the compasses, and found half-a-point difference between the compasses below and those upon deck. The ship answered her helm, and steered like a fish; and I do not hesitate to state that I believed her to be the fastest ship afloat. When a breeze sprung up and the sails were set, by the steamtug's capacity, which I knew to be ten knots an hour, I found that the ship was leaving her at the rate of three or four miles an hour, thus making the speed of the ship from thirteen to fourteen knots an hour. An extraordinary circumstance took place when the steam-tug came up to the ship, to take those parties on shore who had gone out to see their friends off, in-

A contemporary newspaper, from the birthplace of *'Tayleur'*, reports the disaster.

Charles Tayleur, founder of the Vulcan Engineering Works and partner in the Bank Quay Foundry, Warrington.

Chapter One: "The Maddest Pursuit"

Thomas Carlyle observed that, "Of all the mad pursuits any people ever took up, gold digging was the maddest and the stupidest." Certainly, something approaching dementia occurred in mid-nineteenth century Britain when gold was discovered in Australia. Gold! The news of gold being found in unbelievable quantities in New South Wales and in Victoria spread like a bush fire.

In Australia in 1851 gold fever amounted to delirium. There began a veritable stampede from the towns and from the outback as labourers, clerks, artisans and dock workers joined sheep shearers, harvesters and cattlemen in the rush to the goldfields. Seamen deserted their ships, customs officials and policemen left their posts. Shopkeepers and teachers were followed by lawyers and doctors and even by some clergymen – all of them certain that they would make a quick fortune. Every man, woman and child in Australia was affected by gold mania as the price of food and services soared to unprecedented levels because of the acute shortage of labour.

The finds were sensational and new deposits were discovered almost daily. One digger found gold worth £1,800 in a single day. Within a year the population of Melbourne rose from 23,000 to nearly 70,000 and the city was in a state of chaos for months. News of the discoveries swept round the world and in eighteen months the port of Gelong increased from 8,000 inhabitants to 200,000 as hordes of diggers arrived from Britain, Europe and America.

In Britain where the spectre of over-population had occupied government thinking since the beginning of the century, the news of the discovery of gold in Australia was most welcome. The Colonial Land and Emigration Commissioners regarded large-scale emigration to be the essential basis of a colonial empire. Some 300,000 people had left the United Kingdom at the time of the great Californian gold rush of 1849 and a similar exodus to Australia would reduce population pressure in English cities and in Ireland as well as increasing colonial settlement and creating markets for British goods in Australia.

The demand for berths for the voyage to Australia could not be satisfied. There were not enough ships available. From all over Britain and Europe would-be emigrants arrived at British ports seeking passage to Melbourne. Liverpool was foremost among the emigrant ports and the local shipowners endeavoured to cope with demand by diverting vessels which were employed in their Indian and China trades to the Australia route. They also bought and chartered fast American trans-Atlantic clippers and placed orders for new ships with builders in Canada and New England. Every major British shipbuilding yard prospered as the demand for large sailing vessels never slackened. Gold fever even influenced ship design. Speed was essential and the new clipper ships were built to attain the highest speed possible as they were driven to the limit across the stormy Atlantic and Indian oceans.

As the news from the goldfields spread, a vast movement of mainly poor folk began. In one month in 1853 no less than 32,000 people left the port of Liverpool bound for Australia. For about ninety days they were herded together amidst baggage and provisions enduring endless misery as they were tossed about and stifled under battened-down hatches. Weary, sick and soon longing for the homes and the relatives they had left behind, the passengers focussed their thoughts on the wealth they believed that they would undoubtedly acquire within a few months of landing in Australia. After all, it was a well-known fact that the first ship to bring gold from the colony in August 1852 had brought bullion worth £50,000 and the crew had told of labourers in Melbourne who had swaggered about displaying rolls of banknotes. Yet within two years the £50,000 would be regarded as a trifling sum when compared with amounts landed from other vessels. On 17th February 1854 the *Liverpool Mercury* reported that the steamer *Great Britain* had arrived from Sydney with gold valued at £657,850.

Zealous gold diggers.
A family enterprise. Bendigo, Victoria, Australia. 1852.

The abominable voyage could be endured. It would soon pass and be forgotten and a prosperous future was certain. Small wonder that the Mersey docks were crowded with thousands of English, Irish, Scottish and European folk all destined for an antipodean El Dorado.

Gold! The accounts of the sensational finds reached even the most isolated communities in an amazingly short time. Vine dressers in remote valleys in France, Danish fishermen, peat cutters in Prussia, Austrian salt miners and kelp burners in the north of Scotland, all heard within days of the finds being reported in the newspapers.

The gold strikes came at a time of great social change in Britain. The new factories were making many ancient trades obsolete. Machine-made products were bringing a rapid decline in old crafts. Handloom weavers, file-cutters, nailmakers, ropemakers and the makers of hand tools were not required in the new industrial society of the 1850's. As the railway network advanced across the country so carters, farriers, stablemen and turnpike workers lost their jobs. It was the age of coal and iron but not every rural worker wanted to slave in the mills and factories or dwell in town slums. Ploughboys, cowmen, pedlars, gardeners, grave diggers and farm labourers who were used to an outdoor life of privation and long hours were electrified at the news from Australia. Gold was to be found in extraordinary quantities and they determined to have their share. Australia was a new land which welcomed hardy workers. The intending emigrant reasoned that there would be plenty of work even if they did not succeed as prospectors.

Gold caused an exodus of tough Cornish tin miners, railway navvies, Thames lightermen and builders' labourers, all selling everything they possessed to pay for the passage to Australia. They were joined by the failed shopkeeper, the effete ledger clerk, the poacher and the pickpocket. Groups of single girls were caught up in the tide of emigration. Dairymaids, dressmakers, house servants and kitchen scullions all endeavouring to escape lives of poverty and monotony. Gold fever infected even those working folk who were loyal to enlightened employers and those who had a great love of their country and locality.

Of the great press of humanity which hastened to leave the country, most left from the quays of Liverpool. The gold rushes also brought about an enormous expansion in Britain's overseas commerce and industry. The volume of the country's exports far exceeded those of any country in the world and the major part of this traffic was transported through the bustling port of Liverpool.

Despite their efforts in chartering and buying vessels from American owners and builders, the Emigration Commissioners and the Liverpool ship-owners were unable to find the tonnage needed to accommodate the hordes clamouring for passage to Australia. New vessels were urgently required but the building of a large wooden ship was a slow business and time was money. The shipowners knew that the situation could change. It was quite possible that within a year or two the goldfields could be worked out and as a consequence, emigration would be drastically reduced. The early acquisition of new ships was essential if the shipping companies were to capitalise on the demand for berths to Australia.

It was the very discovery of gold thousands of miles away which hastened dramatic changes in British shipbuilding techniques and which helped to solve the ship owners problems. The iron ship was the answer.

Small iron vessels had been build in Britain since the 1830's but they were still a rarity twenty years later. When Brunel's iron steamer, *Great Britain* ran aground on the Irish coast she survived six months battering by the winter gales which would have reduced a wooden ship to matchwood. When the *Great Britain* was refloated it was discovered that she was little damaged. The incident had a profound effect upon the shipbuilding industry and from about 1850 a number of major yards changed from constructing wooden ships to building vessels of iron. The clop of the caulkers' mallets gave way to the din of the riveters' hammers.

Since the earliest times ships had been made of oak but by the beginning of the nineteenth century Britain's ancient forests had been drastically reduced. Besides the timber required for shipbuilding, hardwood was needed for house building, for furniture and for charcoal for metal working. The woods and hedgerows of Old England were rapidly losing their highly prized trees. It was obvious that suitable timber for ships' frames would soon become exhausted and with Britain's naval and mercantile fleets expanding, a suitable substitute for oak had to be found.

It was James Nasmyth's invention of the great steamhammer which made possible the rapid manufacture of iron plating and girders which led to the introduction of the iron ship. These new sailing vessels helped the British Merchant Marine to dominate world shipping and they ended the supremacy of the fast American clipper ships.

The 1850's was the decade of the great clippers which captured the public imagination for their beauty and speed. Before the advent of the clipper ship a passenger could expect his voyage to Australia to take a hundred and twenty days at least. The new greyhounds of the sea were capable of nearly halving that time. The Liverpool gold clippers were usually destined for Melbourne sailing non-stop and out of sight of land between their departure from Britain and the first landfall at Cape Otway at the entrance to the Bass Strait. The ships were household names in Australia.

Emigrant Ships in Melbourne in 1850

Chapter Two: Warrington. A Shipbuilding Town

Warrington is a most unlikely place for the establishment of a shipbuilding industry. The town is about twenty miles east of deep water at the Mersey estuary. The upper reaches of the river from Hale Head to Warrington are shallow and twisting and above Runcorn Gap, the river narrows to become a meandering channel. Today, the mudflats and sandbanks make river traffic to Warrington impossible for craft of any size.

During the early years of the last century there were sailing barges operating to Bank Quay at Warrington. These Mersey "flats" carried sand to Robinson's glassworks, barley to Greenall's brewery and grain to the Warrington millers. George Crosfield, the soap manufacturer, maintained that he carried some six thousand tons of raw material to his Warrington works via the toll-free Mersey. He claimed that it was possible for the river flats to operate to his factory on two hundred days a year. However, by 1830 river traffic was in rapid decline. At the beginning of the century there had been nearly a hundred small craft using the river but by 1850 river conditions had so deteriorated that only about ten boats remained to carry goods to Warrington.

Some idea of the perverse state of the navigable channel in the upper Mersey can be found in a report by Sir John Rennie who in 1840, surveyed the river to explore the feasibility of making a ship canal to Manchester. Of the difficult approaches to Warrington Sir John said, "The largest vessels which can navigate the Mersey from Liverpool to Bank Quay, Warrington, draw about eight to nine feet of water and are eighty to a hundred tons burden but vessels of this class can only come up to Bank Quay at high water of spring tides and even then, unless assisted by a favourable wind or steam tug, they cannot get from Liverpool on one tide."

If a diminutive 60-ton Mersey flat could navigate only with difficulty up this tortuous river to Warrington, how was it possible to launch from the Bank Quay shipyard great ocean-going ships which were the largest merchant sailing vessels of their time? Yet, in spite of it being situated on a capricious river with a twisting and shallow sailing channel, Warrington became, for a brief period, a major centre for the construction of large iron ships.

In the summer of 1853 there was considerable excitement in Warrington at the sight of a very large ship being built on the north bank of the Mersey. The vessel was enormous and passengers travelling through the town by railway wondered how and where the ship would be launched. Bank Quay was a considerable distance from the sea and from the train the passengers could not see water. Most assumed that the ship would be dismantled then reassembled and launched from a slipway near the sea. After all, iron churches, houses and bridges were being prefabricated before being shipped out to the colonies. Undoubtedly, the ship would be launched elsewhere. But this was not to be the case. The great ship was to take to the water from the Bank Quay yard where there could be eighteen feet of water at exceptional spring tides. Furthermore, she was to be launched up the Mersey on a straight stretch of river where she could run for nearly half a mile if this was necessary.

The Warrington Regatta in early Victorian times. The shallow river appears to be too narrow for the event. Warrington was a most unlikely place for the establishment of a shipbuilding industry.

The ship was to have been launched on the first day of September with her fittings, cabins and figurehead being completed in Liverpool. However, there was a late change of plan and it was decided that the vessel would be completed in

Warrington. As a consequence, the date of the launch was put back for a month, the new launch date being the fourth of October.

The ship was to be named *Tayleur* after Charles Tayleur, who with George Sanderson, had established the foundry on the bank of the Mersey near to the London and North Western Railway Station. The partners were fortunate in being able to attract skilled labour to their works for there was a long tradition of metal working in the region. Charles Tayleur was an engineer and entrepreneur of considerable prominence. He was the founder of the world famous Vulcan locomotive works established a few miles away at Newton-le-Willows in 1830. Tayleur amassed a great fortune from his enterprises and over the years he employed many designers and managers who later became famous Victorian engineers in their own right. George Stephenson's son, Robert, was one eminent railway engineer who was associated with the Vulcan works.

Tayleur's connections with the Newton-le-Willows foundry enabled him to muster a skilled workforce at his Bank Quay shipyard in a very short space of time.

Tayleur and Company's Bank Quay Foundry had established a reputation for the manufacture of cannon for the Royal Navy, for making heavy castings and forgings and the works also gained considerable prestige in supplying sections of the Britannia Tubular Railway Bridge which was built across the Menai Straits. Within four years of its foundation the firm's name was further enhanced when a huge hydraulic press manufactured at Bank Quay was awarded a diploma at the Great Exhibition of 1851.

Since the early 1840's iron barges had been used on the Mersey. These proved to be satisfactory in every respect and in 1846 Tayleur and Co. launched, on the same tide, two small iron schooners each of about seventy-five tons. A couple of years later the partners extended the shipyard by leasing more land and an ambitious but short-lived programme of ship construction began. The Bank Quay company pioneered the building of the largest iron ocean-going sailing ships.

Tayleur's dimensions were staggering. She was the largest merchant sailing ship built in England up to that time and her tonnage was not to be surpassed by a merchant sailing vessel for another six years. She was built for the Liverpool firm of Charles Moore and Company and was chartered by Pilkington and Wilson for their White Star Line of Australian clippers. William Rennie of Messrs. Rennie, Johnson and Company of Liverpool designed the ship. Rennie was an outstanding designer of iron ships and certainly no other naval architect is better known for clipper design.

William Rennie had acquired vast experience in shipbuilding yards in Aberdeen; in Bathhurst, New Brunswick, Canada and in Liverpool. He was consulted by shipbuilders from all over the country drawing the plans for vessels launched in London, Dundee, Dumbarton and Troon. Undoubtedly, Rennie was Britain's foremost designer of fast merchant ships.

Just as work on the vessel was about to commence, the dimensions of the ship were enlarged. Her length was increased by twenty feet to two hundred and twenty-five feet and her beam was increased by four feet to forty feet. The depth of the hull was twenty-eight feet. There was an assertion that the original plan was for the vessel to have been a screw-driven steamer and that the original hull design had remained unchanged. It was rumoured that the *Tayleur* was a hybrid – a sailing vessel with a steamer's hull. Whatever the truth, the ship had an impressive cargo-carrying capacity. She could carry over four thousand tons of cargo and she had accommodation for six hundred and eighty passengers.

For about twenty years the commercial and manufacturing activity of Warrington had stagnated. The town had not grown at the same pace as many other towns in the region, most of which had outstripped Warrington in population growth. The local press had bemoaned the decline in the town's economic fortune with factories departing to more favourable locations. Now however, the future was bright. The railway network through Warrington was almost complete with connections to London, Liverpool, Manchester and the manufacturing towns of the Midlands. There were grounds for optimism. The *Warrington Guardian* noted; "We have sent our factories to Preston and our public works to Crewe. We may shut up our baths, ignore our adult schools, determined to do without a closed market, be perfectly sure that our streets need no improvement and our roads need no change but still fortune smiles on us." The newspaper invited its readers to visit Bank Quay, "Where the Mersey indolently winds against a background of wooded Cheshire hills – to see in still meadows a vessel rising to astonish Liverpool and even make the shipbuilders of our generation look grave." In the town there was exultation at the probability of large scale manufacturing increasing at Bank Quay and the yard's heightened activity prompted the *Guardian* to note that in addition to the recently completed work for the Menai Railway bridge, Tayleur and Company were building two locomotives for Indian railways and another for a railway in Canada. The foundry was also engaged in making fluted iron columns for Bass's large bitter beer warehouse in Wapping as well as manufacturing a bridge to cross the Mersey for the railway being built between Altrincham and Warrington. Even before half the work on *Tayleur* had been completed came the news that the yard had secured the contract to build another ship of similar dimensions as well as two smaller vessels. Undoubtedly, the future of manufacturing was assured and the newspaper confidently expressed the view that; "The Bank Quay Foundry Company is well-known outside Great Britain and a tide is now floating Warrington into a sea of enterprise and giving us a chance with the commercial cities of the world." Before long it was stated, all ships would be made of iron and soon Warrington would rival Sunderland and Clydeside in ship construction.

An Invoice heading of Charles Tayleur's Vulcan engineering works at Newton-le Willows, near Warrington.

Optimism was the mood of the time but there were some who doubted the practicability of large ship construction at Bank Quay. The *Warrington Guardian* article considered the fickle, shallow and winding sailing channel in the upper river to be a minor difficulty. It pointed out that, "The Clyde was as unsuitable for shipbuilding as is the Mersey between Runcorn and Warrington but the enterprise of the Glasgow citizens has overcome all the natural difficulties and at the present time there are sixty iron vessels in progress of building along its banks at as great a distance from the sea as is Warrington."

Charles Tayleur and George Sanderson were fully aware of the problems involved in getting a large ship down the intricate Mersey channel. They sought the advice of a Mr. James Leigh who was familiar with the vacillating conditions of the upper river. Leigh was certain that the project was possible and he suggested that

Captain James Foulkes of the Bridgewater Trustees should supervise the operation. Leigh also advised the partners to employ only Runcorn tug-boat masters who were used to towing on the upper Mersey.

The local press continued to exude confidence in Warrington's industrial future pointing out that iron ships meant that the new shipyards would be established near foundries and coalfields. Warrington was ideally situated being equidistant from the Lancashire coalfield and the Staffordshire foundries with excellent rail links to both sources of supply.

On 17th September the local newspaper reported on the progress being made on the *Tayleur*. Besides giving details of her construction, an article proclaimed the undoubted advantages gained when using iron. There was no disputing the fact that iron vessels were much stronger than wooden ones. They could stand unlimited pounding into a head sea. Iron masts were stronger than those made of wood and wire stays were far superior to the thick, clumsy rope shrouds used in wooden ships. It was a fact that the iron vessel did not suffer the many small leaks which were endemic in the wooden ship caused by the constant working of the planks in heavy seas. Furthermore, iron ships were cheaper to build because they could be constructed quickly by a small workforce. Then there was the question of cargo-carrying capacity. Here, the iron vessel had more storage space. Because of the massive frames that were needed to strengthen a wooden ship, her cargo holds were reduced. The newspaper article claimed that the new clipper could carry nearly twice the tonnage of a wooden-hulled vessel of the same size.

The *Warrington Guardian* statements which proclaimed the advantages in using iron were irrefutable but there were also drawbacks. For instance, the hull of an iron ship could not be treated with a satisfactory anti-fouling agent to inhibit the accumulation of marine growth which slowed her speed. The hulls of wooden vessels were sheathed in yellow metal which retarded marine growth. However, there was another, far more serious disadvantage incurred when using iron – that of compass deviation which could lure an iron ship to disaster. It was believed that Brunel's *Great Britain* was stranded on the Irish coast when her master was deceived by false compass readings. Even though many shipowners were buying the new iron vessels there were some who hesitated to place orders because of the growing evidence of shipwreck caused by disordered compasses. But there were no references to this threatening phenomena in the local press. The scene in Warrington was one of pride, exultation and wonder.

As the great ship neared completion the local newspapers rapturously listed her qualities. It was claimed that *Tayleur* was the mightiest merchant sailing ship ever built. She was a first-class vessel in every respect. She would prove to be the strongest, the fastest and the most comfortable clipper ship afloat. No expense had been spared in her construction. She was a ship of superior build and was classified A1 at Lloyds.

The newspapers made much of the *Tayleur's* great strength and also the spacious quarters for the crew and the passengers. She was indeed, supreme amongst the sailing ships of the world. The *Tayleur* would outclass every emigrant ship on the Australia route. Her future success was certain.

The press reported, "This splendid, first-class sailing vessel is to be built, completed and delivered to Liverpool within six months of her keel being laid down." The account set out the features of the ship's structure in some detail, "She has three decks with a camboose (saloon) on the upper deck and a saloon with cabins and berths for the captain and principal officers. She is double riveted throughout and well over-lapped and will be the strongest craft afloat being divided into five water-tight compartments each fitted with pumps. She has an enormous box keelson running fore and aft (two feet six inches by two feet) which will carry twenty-five tons of water with a pump at one end to render it available for use, whilst in the meantime it will serve as a ballast. The beams are of great strength and are only twelve feet apart, the beams to the lower deck being nine inches deep and half an inch thick. Her frames are all of angle-iron five inches by three inches and five-eighths of an inch thick with reverse frames also of angle-iron, three inches by three inches. These are fifteen inches apart amidships and eighteen inches apart fore and aft. The girders which support her floorings are very massive and were more like those of a bridge in strength being provided with "L" shaped flanges on the top to receive the ceilings. The plating at the vessel's keel was an inch thick and on most of the hull it was three-quarters of an inch in thickness."

Life aboard a crowded emigrant ship in heavy weather was one of intense misery. Sea sick and home sick, the young and old of many nations were packed together in semi-darkness. Equally distressing was the slow passage through the doldrums. Between decks in tropical waters the passengers' accommodation was airless and stifling. The heat could be almost beyond endurance resulting in illness and countless fights and quarrels. However, the ventilation arrangements for the *Tayleur* were excellent. "Her beam is forty feet – unusually great being ten feet wider than other vessels of this class engaged in this trade. She is very lofty and her ventilation is perfect. A shaft throughout her foretopgallant deck and four portholes in her stern afford a constant current of air and she has besides, seven covered hatchways with windows to open and close and side-lights about eight feet apart along her whole length and opening into every berth. In every respect the ship is a perfect model of what an emigrant ship ought to be. Without doubt she will prove herself worthy of the great skills, pains and liberal expense which have been bestowed on her."

The crew's quarters were claimed to be superior to those on any other ship and as for the passenger accommodation, it was spacious, well ventilated with skylights to ensure maximum light below deck and between decks there was a clearance of six feet seven inches.

Whilst it was acknowledged that the *Tayleur* did not have the sharp lines of most of the recently built clippers, "It is expected that she will be very stiff under canvas and a very swift sailer." The ship would have a huge spread of sail. The lower masts were ninety-four feet long, made of iron with traverse strengthening plates inside running from top to bottom. The fore and main yards were eighty-four feet long. There was only a brief reference to the ship's rudder, which was simply described as being "a patent design".

The large galleys were situated at the fore part of the vessel and they, "Matched the same superior comfort and conveniences to be found on passenger steamers". For the first class passengers accommodation was provided in the saloon on deck. A few days before she was due to take to the water, the ship's figurehead – a full-length representation of Charles Tayleur, was fitted and on the stern was his family crest and other emblems.

The total cost of building the ship amounted to £34,000. She was part insured with companies in Liverpool and in Glasgow for £25,000.

Chapter Three: The Launch of the *Tayleur*

The day of the launch, Tuesday, 4th October dawned with overcast skies but the morning remained dry as thousands made their way towards the Bank Quay yard to witness the launch of the much-vaunted clipper. The shops closed early, as at mid-day, the crowds took up positions on Warrington Bridge and along the southern bank of the river.

The local press reported, "All classes contributed to the crowd. The councillor was there with that expression of senatorial gravity, which a year in office never fails to give. The merchant was there proud of the day which promised so much for Warrington, the tradesman glad of a holiday that looked like a pledge for increased trade, artisans, mechanics and labourers of all kinds thronged to view the vessel which was about to grace her proper element. Wives and daughters came, some in carriages with gloved hands clasped in earnest admiration. The sweethearts and partners of many a rough but honest fellow came to scream their pretty cries of delight. The foundry yard was full of laughing life whilst steamers on the river freighted hundreds."

On the slipway *Tayleur* was aligned with her bows pointing north towards a spur of the Pennine Hills. The bunting-draped stage for the principal guests at the launching ceremony was at the stern of the ship with other platforms erected at the sides of the stocks.

When the tide had almost reached its full height at 1.20pm there came the sound of rhythmic hammering as the blocks were knocked away. To deafening applause Miss Patten, the daughter of Wilson Patten, the M.P. for North Lancashire, broke a bottle of christening wine against the ship's stern and inch by inch the vessel moved towards the water. In their eagerness to obtain a better view some dignified and elderly gentlemen actually clambered across scaffolding poles and up ladders to balance themselves on girders whilst holding on to coping stones.

Opposite the foundry the crush of spectators was such that many were stood on the very edge of the river bank. There were screams of laughter as the launch wave surged towards the crowd soaking a hundred spectators. Men hoisted girls upon their shoulders and policemen helped many people to regain a foothold. Some spectators found themselves standing in water up to their knees. "Many of the weaker vessels as the sex is called, were literally floating. Sober tee-totallers half seas over and men, guiltless of having a bath before now underwent the water cure." Fortunately, there were no injuries.

The launch was so clean that it took everyone by surprise. Within seconds the ship was floating gracefully on the river. As she drew up at the bank-side there was a great roar of applause and admiration. She then slowly turned to display her whole length to the spectators.

It was vital that no time should be lost. Speed was essential in order that the *Tayleur* could be conveyed safely over the shallows at Fiddlers Ferry whilst the tide was at its height.

Within a couple of minutes the attending paddle-tugs had secured the vessel. Then towed by *Victory* with *Gleaner* lashed to one side of the ship and *Reaper* to the other, the clipper, ballasted with a hundred tons of coal, was taken down river at the height of the flood.

After the launch the honoured guests were invited into the works where they took refreshments supplied from the 'Patten Arms'. Not all the principal spectators were in attendance for some, including his worship the Mayor of Warrington, Mr. Joseph Perrin, had gone aboard a steamer which had followed the *Tayleur* to Runcorn.

Among the dignitaries present in the foundry were most of the town's clergy including the Honourable and Reverend Horace Powys, the Reverend Henry Bostock, the Reverend Richard Greenall, the Reverend John Kay and the Reverend E.J. Hartland. The Town Clerk and Mr. William Beaumont, the noted local historian were also present with Mr. H.C. Moore representing the ship's owners.

On behalf of the owners Mr. Moore proposed the health of, "All the members of the firm of the Bank Quay Foundry." He said that his company were so impressed by the skill and energy of the foundry workforce they were prepared to leave all the details of construction and launch to Tayleur and Company and the result had proved that they were right in placing confidence in the shipyard. Mr. Moore said that the launch had been a glorious occasion and he had no doubt that the ship would earn well deserved praise for her construction and fine lines at the port of Liverpool. To loud applause he thanked and congratulated the Bank Quay Company and he predicted that the ship would receive a welcome in Australia where she would, "Give another proof to the children of that country that their fathers had not forgotten the art of shipbuilding."

Mr. Heathcote, the foundry manager, acknowledged the warm manner in which the health of the firm had been received and in a brief but heart-felt speech he returned the thanks of his company.

The occasion had been a splendid spectacle for the thousands who had turned out to watch the launch but there was a sad note to the proceedings. Charles Tayleur, after whom the ship was named, was not present at the ceremony for, a few days before the launch his wife had died. Furthermore, the occasion could have been blighted by tragedy when, the day before the launch, Captain John Noble, *Tayleur*'s master, fell twenty-five feet into the ship's hold and astonishingly escaped serious injury. He was however, unfit to attend the launching ceremony and was unable to command the vessel for the short journey to Liverpool.

The rain began just as the assembled guests were leaving the platforms in the shipyard. The flags and the bunting hung dejectedly as the crowd hurried away to seek shelter when the weather became wretched. In the meantime, a couple of miles downstream *Tayleur* was approaching danger as the tugs were having difficulty in controlling the vessel in the narrow, twisting channel near Fiddlers Ferry.

The approach of the ship and her tugs was witnessed by John Corbett, a pupil at the Society of Friends (Quaker) school in Penketh. Corbett was to become the Borough Engineer of Salford and writing nearly fifty years after the event, he recalled the excitement of the spectacle. With his classmates and their teacher, Corbett was waiting on the bank of the Sankey Canal which enters the Mersey at Fiddlers Ferry. For months the boys had watched the ship being constructed. They had seen the skeleton being clad with plating and the distant sound of the riveters at work could be heard every day. They had been eagerly awaiting the launch and now suddenly, the great ship was bearing down upon them.

Corbett writes graphically of the tugs struggling to manoeuvre the ship round a sharp bend in the river. "I was frightened by the sight of the high, sharp bows of the ship close at hand and apparently rushing straight at us. My alarm was warranted by real circumstances for the pilot had underestimated his difficulty in turning the bend. The consequences were nearly being very serious for the great ship swung close to the sloping river bank just above the lock wall where we were and she pushed the little starboard tug right up the bank." Strong hawsers snapped like threads as *Tayleur* came near to driving onto the masonry of the lock wall on which the boys were sitting but then the port side tug went astern on full power, control was regained and with a few feet clearance, the ship passed rapidly down river to the relief of the shocked spectators.

There then occurred a remarkable example of sound, quick judgement and prompt execution of orders for which the Victorian workforce was noted. Even before *Tayleur* was out of sight strenuous efforts had been commenced in order to refloat the stranded tug.

A short distance from the river the Manchester to Garston railway was under construction and hundreds of navvies with their foremen and the engineer in charge were watching the ship pass by. When the tug was pushed up on to the bank and the ship nearly followed her there was a loud cry of alarm but Corbett records; "Almost immediately a loud, firm voice announced the scheme of the clear-headed engineer and with instant obedience, the navvies ran to piles of slender scaffold poles that lay fifty yards away and brought them at a run to the waterside; every moment was valuable with the tide running down so fast. Each pole was grasped by a score of strong men. Many scores of poles worked side by side as methodically as if they had been drilled for this special work. The poles were thrust against the side of the tugboat and at the word of command, all together, they thrust the hundred-ton tug down the sloping bank and into the water, many of the men wading deeply to make the thrust more effective and in far less time than it takes to tell, the tug was paddling along at her best speed to overtake the ship to resume her duty."

Tayleur, by now followed by a procession of small craft containing spectators, approached the village of Moore. Far away to the south, across Moore Marshes, the long range of the mountains of North Wales tapered away to the southern horizon. A few days previously the marshes had provided pasture for scores of cattle. Now they had become great lagoons which had increased the Mersey to three times its normal width.

The river's natural deep channel had been carefully marked by Captain James Foulkes, the Superintendent of Lights and Buoys to the Trustees of the Duke of Bridgewater's Navigation who had taken on the responsibility of plotting the navigable channel of the upper Mersey. For months Foulkes had used the little paddle-tug *Tower* to site perhaps a hundred miniature buoys and a number of perches to mark the eight miles of winding channel from Warrington to Runcorn. As the great ship approached the low-lying Moore village she appeared to be sailing over the fields before plunging into woods, her tall masts and spars reappearing as if by magic a moment later.

Throughout the last century the upper Mersey at high tide always resembled a regatta with dozens of single mast sailing flats working to the Sankey Canal, to the Old Quay docks at Runcorn or to those of the Bridgewater Trustees. As the tugs conveyed the *Tayleur* to where the river widened into a basin between

Cuerdley and Norton on the Cheshire bank, there were no small craft to be seen. The ship and her tugs had been allowed complete freedom to operate unhindered by other traffic on the river.

The ebb tide was quickening as the flood waters off the marshes carried the clipper towards the narrows of Runcorn Gap. The villagers of Halton had a long view of *Tayleur's* approach. From the top of Halton Hill with its ruined castle they were able to observe the ship's progress almost from the moment of her launch. As she neared the Gap at Runcorn, the ship glided past the locks and docks of the Mersey and Irwell Navigation Company's Old Quay Canal. Here, the dock labourers and flatmen cheered her to the echo. Adjacent to the Old Quay docks was the shipyard of Brundrit and Company from which, a few weeks previously, the wooden ship *Anne Chesshyre,* the largest vessel ever built at Runcorn, had been launched. *Tayleur's* displacement was four times that of *Anne Chesshyre.*

In spite of the incessant rain it seemed that all of Runcorn's seven thousand inhabitants had assembled along the river's edge and a carnival atmosphere prevailed. On the opposite bank of the river, at rural Widnes, soon to be devastated by the spread of chemical works and waste tips, the men from the new factories came to cheer as did folk from as far afield as Prescot and St. Helens.

At Runcorn Gap, once the site of a Saxon fortress which was built at the narrows to deter Viking longships from venturing up river, the Mersey is less than a quarter of a mile wide. As the ship came into view the crowds were over-awed by her size. Standing high on the tide, she was enormous. Her masts soared as high as the steeple of Runcorn's newly-built Parish Church.

Before Runcorn Gap was bridged in 1868 the only means of crossing the river was by a rowing-boat ferry. At low water the ferry-boats were often stranded on sandbanks in mid-stream. To overcome this problem serious consideration was given to a plan to equip the boats with wheels in order that they could be hauled across the sand. This curious amphibious craft never became a reality but the wags in the Runcorn beerhouses contended that the only way that *Tayleur* could be brought down this stretch of shallow water was by fitting her with enormous wheels. However, all doubts were proved baseless when the ship cleared the hidden menace of the Hurst Rocks and the Church Bank to reach a deep gutter in the channel near the mouth of Ditton Brook. Here the ship was anchored. As there was no room in the narrow channel to allow the vessel to swing with the tide and as she was drawing eight and a half feet of water, she was anchored fore and aft. Positioned near by, the Bridgewater Trustees' little light vessel, *Plutas,* was

A photograph of 1860 showing low water at Runcorn Gap. The Hurst Rocks presented a considerable risk to 'Tayleur' on her passage down river.

keeping a watching brief.

With *Tayleur* safe at anchor the river came to life. Suddenly the Mersey swarmed with small craft. There were shrimping boats carrying sight-seers, sailing flats and spindly funnelled paddle-tugs towing trains of barges to and from Liverpool.

Having seen the ship secure the tugs left taking with them the privileged passengers who had travelled down river from Bank Quay. A couple of hours later, at low water, there was not another vessel to be seen. Apart from *Plutas*, the great clipper was alone in the narrow channel which now wound its way through miles of sandbanks and mudflats to the sea.

As darkness descended on the silent ship it was recreation time in the Quaker school in Penketh. After an exciting day the boys were occupied with hobbies and games. One boy, however, made a vivid drawing of *Tayleur* swamped by heavy seas as she lay wrecked under steep cliffs. His classmates were angry. They seized the offending drawing and tore it to pieces. The picture was unworthy, despicable, an insult. In any case such a disaster was impossible for was not their *Tayleur* the strongest sailing ship ever built? It had been a perfect day and the boys were not going to allow Jim Thompson to spoil the occasion with his shameful scribbling.

Before nine o'clock next morning the tugs arrived to take *Tayleur* on to Liverpool. At vantage points on Runcorn Hill, Frodsham Hill and from the waterfront at Weston Point hundreds of spectators had gathered all eager to see the largest sailing vessel ever built pass down river before setting out on her maiden voyage to Australia. It was a day to be remembered.

The ship was towed past the Runcorn Bridgewater Docks with the tall warehouse and the neat piles of potters' materials which had been brought from Cornwall and Devon in the dozens of coastal schooners crowding the docks. Ships' crews and dock workers lined the piers as the leviathan slipped by. It was cheering, waving and clapping until she was out of sight.

Near the confluence of the Weaver and Mersey rivers the spire of the neo-gothic church of Christ Church, Weston Point, rose above the masts of the shipping in the Weaver Docks. The church was built on the quayside for the flatmen and narrowboat men and their families. Its steeple provided a useful aid to navigation for coastal craft working to Runcorn and Weston Point but during the evening services the church lamps had to be masked as they could be mistaken for shore lights. The ship then entered the wide inner estuary between Frodsham and Hale. At Hale Head the Mersey widens out to one and a half miles. For some years the river's ever-changing deep channel had been gradually shifting its course from the Cheshire shore towards the northern bank. This migration of the channel afforded those spectators who had gathered near Hale Head lighthouse the opportunity of seeing the *Tayleur* at close quarters.

The old lighthouse and 'keeper's cottage at Hale Head.

At Hale the atmosphere is one of light, space and tranquillity. Even today, a century and a half after the passing of the great ship, the area is still one of rural peace with cultivated fields reaching to the shoreline. On the morning of *Tayleur's* appearance, however, there was considerable activity and excitement.

The appearance of a 150-ton vessel on this stretch of river was a very rare sight. At two thousand tons the *Tayleur* was colossal, overwhelming, beyond belief. The towering masts and great spars dwarfed the little lighthouse and keeper's cottage. For a brief moment the sight-seers were able to admire the ship's elegant lines. In reply to the cheers of the spectators men waved from the ship's deck and from the yards. The huge ram of the bowsprit and the figurehead of Charles Tayleur swept by as the ship was conveyed down the buoyed channel towards a crowd waiting on the long abandoned salt refinery wharf at Dungeon Point. Smoke from the tug drifted across the fields. At Oglet and Garston Docks the mighty vessel received a tumultuous reception. A few minutes later the ship had reached deep water at the port of Liverpool. Her safe arrival there was telegraphed to Mr. Heathcote at the Bank Quay yard at eleven o'clock.

It had been a day to remember and a great triumph for all those who had been involved in building the ship. Captain Foulkes was the hero of the hour. The Superintendent of Lights and Buoys had taken the great vessel down the capricious Mersey without her receiving a scratch. The management of the shipyard was prompt in placing a notice in the *Warrington Guardian* thanking Foulkes and his men for the efficient manner in which the operation had been conducted.

Not everyone rejoiced at Captain Foulkes' success however. James Leigh who had recommended Foulkes for command had been on the towing tug and he had a role to play in the journey down river. From the start of the tow the two men did not see eye to eye. Leigh thought that Foulkes' system of signalling with flags, "Was perfectly useless." He also believed that Foulkes had been wrong to place one of the ship's anchors on Ditton Marsh, "Because this was unnecessary and if he had understood the matter better he would have saved the firm near £50." Leigh envied Foulkes for the acclaim the captain had merited and a week after the launch he wrote a sour letter to the local newspaper in which he claimed he had played a role of equal importance. In his letter Leigh stated that for his valuable service during the towage operation he had been awarded five pounds by the Bank Quay Company. Mr Leigh's complaint was the only discordant note to be sounded on the occasion of the triumphant event.

Chapter Four: The Crew, the Passengers and the Cargo

The directors of the White Star Line were proud of their new clipper and in newspaper advertisements they declared. "This truly splendid vessel and the largest merchantman ever built in England will undoubtedly prove to be the fastest of the Australian fleet as she has been constructed expressly with the object of attaining the very highest rate of speed. Her vast dimensions enable the owners to provide passenger accommodation not to be met with in any vessel afloat. Through ventilation has been secured and, by means of ports of which she has one every seven feet, is perfectly lighted in every part. The undersigned have, therefore, no hesitation, in affirming that the *Tayleur* presents advantages as a passenger conveyance superior to any ship hitherto dispatched to the Australian colonies."

Pilkington and Wilson
Commercial Buildings, Water Street.

All the Liverpool firms engaged in the Australia trade carried on cut-throat competition for business and fast passages were necessary for success in the undertaking. Clipper captains were forced to strain every sail to outstrip the wind in order to achieve record passages. The average time of a voyage from anchorage to anchorage was about ninety days. However, a few months before *Tayleur's* arrival in Liverpool the *Marco Polo* of Baines and Company's Black Ball Line achieved an astonishing voyage of seventy-six days and other vessels had completed the passage in eighty-days. Quick passages also guaranteed good publicity for the newspapers reported the time taken in headlines which suggested that the main purpose of the voyage was the winning of a race.

The masters of the clippers were celebrities and the shipping companies always named their captains in newspaper advertisements and posters. Successful captains often acquired a following when passengers were attracted to a particular vessel because of the master's reputation.

Some of the ships leaving Liverpool for Australia were hired by the Government Emigration Department but these were few compared to the fleet of ships owned by the shipping companies. The greatest rival of the White Star Line was the Black Ball Line but the competition also included the Fox Line of Henry Fox and Company; Millers and Thompson's Golden Line; the Fernie Brothers' Red Cross Line; the Liverpool Thistle Line of Duncan Gibb; the Australian Line of Brice, Friend & Co; Scott and Roxburgh; the Eagle Line of Gibbs, Bright and Co.; and the Liverpool Line of John Starr de Wolf.

By 1850 Liverpool had become one of the greatest ports in the world. Its miles of docks were crowded with hundreds of ocean-going and coastal craft of every type and size. The town depended almost entirely on the sea. The sea was its life and substance for Liverpool was a centre of trade and commerce rather than a place of manufacture and its economy was based on the port.

Passenger traffic to Australia, New Zealand and North America was an important component of the economic activity of the port. Although emigration was seasonal in that most passengers preferred to leave Britain during the summer months so as to avoid the winter storms in northern seas, there was, nevertheless, a continuous demand for berths throughout November, December and January. By April the press reports indicate that over fifty vessels were dispatched from Liverpool under the Emigration Act during the month with another thirty-four preparing to depart. Winter departures had seen *Marco Polo, Salem* and *Essex* achieve record passages and while *Tayleur* was fitting out the newspapers carried dozens of notices offering berths in vessels about to sail. In spite of the onset of winter, emigration continued to dominate shipping news.

On Liverpool's quays, every day saw the arrival of hundreds of bemused emigrants. Escaping from lives of misery and deprivation and buoyed up by pipe-dreams promising the certainty of striking it rich, poor Irish families, Scottish crofters and English labourers came in hordes. They were prepared to face the horrors of weeks below decks during winter storms on the Atlantic. Love of country, family ties, the familiar sights of home and the certainties of life did not restrain them in their haste to be away. A new nation had been established and all the countries of Europe were contributing to its settlement.

Something of the extraordinary flight to the goldfields is conveyed in an evangelical tract which was distributed at the religious services which were held on board emigrant ships just prior to departure, "The exodus still continues. With what eager rapidity one multitude follows another. They have no king, yet their muster is prompt and their march is regular. The great army moves on, its footsteps lead to the sea, its heart meditating battle with the wilderness and the scrub and the uncultivated virgin soil and thirsting for the golden spoil of lands which their fathers knew not."

Among the many clippers which were taking on cargo for Melbourne were *Sumatra, Fitzjames, Emma* and *Lochiel*. Pilkington and Wilson had the *Golden Era and* the *Ben Nevis* both of which were due to sail about the same time as *Tayleur*. The arrival of the new ship from Warrington attracted much attention.

*Advertisements in the 'Liverpool Mercury' giving details of White Star Line sailings
to Australia and New Zealand.*

A mid-Victorian poster advertising White Star Line sailings to Australia.

A Mr. W.G. Lindsay "whose experience in the construction of ships and in shipping affairs gives his remarks some importance", thought that the *Tayleur* was the finest specimen of naval architecture ever produced in Britain. Lindsay took the opportunity to minutely inspect the clipper whilst she was in Bramley-Moore dock. He declared that, "He had never before seen a stronger and finer merchant ship." The ship's elegant lines were described in an article in the *Liverpool Standard*. "She is perceptibly hollow in her entrance and clean in her tail, her bow as well as her stern lines commencing near to midships, whilst her large extent of floor will ensure her carrying a considerable cargo. Her great expanse of canvas will allow her to make rapid way through her destined element."

Tayleur was said to have been similar to the *Sarah Neumann* but broader and deeper with the heavy rounded stern which many iron ships possessed, but she was different from most clippers in that, "she had not much tumblechome", that is she had little angle of inclination in the upper part of her sides. Vessels having this characteristic were often described as being wall-sided. Another report estimated that the ship could load 4,200 tons of cargo on a draught of twenty-one feet. The ship had three decks but passengers were carried on the main deck only, the lower deck and the hold being reserved for cargo.

As soon as *Tayleur* had been tied up in Bramley-Moore dock the work of making her ready for sea in the shortest possible time was begun. There was a great deal to be done before the cargo could be taken on board. The ship needed sails, and rigging, ships' lifeboats, galley fittings, furnishings for the passenger accommodation and for the crew's quarters as well as the great variety of ships' stores and equipment. These preparations would take three and a half months.

It was while the vessel was lying in Bramley-Moore dock that John Gray "compass maker to Her Majesty" went on board her to fit and compensate the three compasses. Gray did not fit the latest azimuth compasses and it is a matter of some surprise that the ship was not equipped with the most up-to-date instruments as Captain Noble had carte blanche from the owners to procure anything that he required before sailing. It is possible however, that the captain needed time to recover from his near fatal accident and that as a consequence, he was not on board the ship to supervise the fitting of the compasses.

Most of the rigging was fitted whilst the ship was in Bramley-Moore dock and every new item of equipment was checked as it was installed. In one instance only was there a lack of inspection and surveillance – that of the *Tayleur*'s sailing abilities. Sea trials for sailing ships were unknown at the time. The vessel's temperament and her merits and foibles would be discovered only after she had put to sea on her first voyage.

European settlement in Australia had begun a mere sixty-five years before the *Tayleur* was to take her complement of emigrants to that country. Every individual and every ton of merchandise destined for the colony had to go by sea. The settlers relied on the mother country for all their manufactured goods and the variety of exports shipped to Melbourne and Sydney was infinite. Everything was in demand and there was an insatiable market for British products of every kind. The clippers left port loaded to capacity – and indeed, often beyond safe loading. Even the ballast material was a saleable commodity. To give a vessel stability heavy material such as building stone, house bricks, paving flags, roofing slates and bar iron were loaded first followed by the great diversity of merchandise needed in the rapidly developing colony. For the return voyage to Britain bales of wool provided the bulk of the ballast cargo.

In the first week in January Pilkington and Wilson's agents gave notice that *Tayleur* was to be moved from Bramley-Moore dock to her loading berth at Salthouse Dock. Intending passengers were notified that, "Luggage must be alongside the vessel tomorrow (Wednesday) and the next two days and passengers to embark on 14th January."

At her loading berth *Tayleur* was surrounded by Liverpool's most impressive buildings – warehouses of enormous size. The great eight storey buildings formed part of a complex of docks with wide quays and graving docks. Herman Melville, the American author of *Moby Dick* fame, was over-awed by the scale of the warehouses which dwarfed any that he had seen in the United States. In strength and durability the vast buildings were unsurpassed and Melville compared them to the pyramids and the Great Wall of China. Equipped with the latest hydraulic machinery, the warehouses were among the wonders of the world. This was the scene which met *Tayleur's* passengers when they arrived at the docks. To the bewildered emigrant newly arrived from his village far from the sea, the quayside must have appeared a chaotic maelstrom with horse-drawn wagons struggling to find a way through a maze of piled casks, crates, luggage and assorted cargo. The clamour of dock labourers, warehousemen and seamen added to the turmoil. Everything seemed to be in disarray. Scores of small craft, barges and tug-boats appeared to be intractably tangled together with tall ships in the limited dock space. Under overcast skies only the ships' figureheads presented a cheerful prospect. These intricate carvings were very handsome. They were gilded and brightly painted each representing a striking feature which instantly identified the vessel. Most figureheads were female but there were mythical sea creatures, Neptunes, mermaids, dolphins and porpoise. In stark contrast to these gay images, the dark figurehead of Charles Tayleur dressed in a frock-coat seemed to brood over the busy scene.

Tayleur's cargo was a large miscellany of all the products of the "Workshop of the World". First to be loaded were thousands of common bricks and roofing slates followed by anvils, sheet lead, bar iron, galvanised iron and six tons of zinc. Then came a cask of rivets, three cast iron cranes, fireplaces, fifteen tons of wire fencing and seven ploughs. Other items included four cases of flint glass, three bundles of cart covers, a box of lamps and lanterns, clothing, hosiery, blankets, bales of cloth, leather, bottled beer, saddles, harness, books, boxes of tinplate, hogsheads of chinaware, a piano, hats and caps and Sicilian wine. The main item of cargo was a large consignment of sawn timber in twenty-eight foot lengths and buried deep in the ship's hold, were about thirty blank gravestones! Even the colonial dead relied on British exports.

The last thing to be hoisted aboard was a small steamboat, fifty feet long and nine feet wide and intended for use on the Australian rivers. The boat was securely fastened to the ship's deck. Its tiny cabin was to be the living quarters for its engineer and his wife for the entire voyage to Melbourne.

During her precarious journey from the shipyard *Tayleur* had a draught of eight and a half feet. Now fully laden the vessel had a draught of seventeen feet forward and eighteen feet three inches aft. She was a floating warehouse and the value of her cargo was estimated to have been over twenty thousand pounds.

Three or four days before the ship was due to sail her crew came aboard. Of the total complement of 71 men who signed articles only one man, the third mate, nineteen year old Hugh Cowan, was known to Captain Noble. In all, there were fifty-five men to work the ship. These included six apprentices, four of whom had never been to sea before. The remaining sixteen crew were listed as passengers' cooks and stewards. Twenty-two crew members could neither read nor write and they "made a mark" when signing on. Fourteen were foreign nationals. They included two Lascars, three Chinese, six men from Trieste, two Greeks and a Dane. The three Chinese could not speak or understand English.

Many of the seamen were recruited from the Sailors' Home in Canning Place which had been built a couple of years previously by subscription from merchants and ship owners so as to provide seamen with a refuge from the prostitutes and beerhouse keepers who could part them from their earnings within hours of them coming ashore. According to Herman Melville, "Of all the seaports in the world, Liverpool perhaps abounds in the variety of land sharks, land rats and other vermin which makes the hapless mariner their prey. Landlords, bar-keepers, clothiers, crimps and boarding house loungers and land sharks devour him limb from limb."

It was a motley crew which assembled a couple of days before *Tayleur* was taken from the dock to her anchorage in the river. By no stretch of the imagination could the disparate group be called a crew. They were a collection of individuals, many of whom had signed on to work the passage out to Australia intending to desert ship at Melbourne before making for the goldfields at Forest Creek, Bendigo, The Ovens or Ararat. The men were taken on without any rigorous probing to ascertain their reliability or their sea-going experience.

From the ship's clearance certificate the status and the pay of the various members of the crew can be ascertained. There were twenty-six able seamen of whom twenty-two were to be paid five pounds a month with the other four receiving three pounds a month. The pay of the ordinary seamen ranged from two pounds fifteen shillings to two pounds a month. The ship's steward who was also required to assist with deck duties, was paid four pounds ten shillings and the ship's cook, two pounds ten shillings a month. The differentials in wages shows that some of the seamen were not yet out of their time. One of the passengers noted that the younger members of the crew "were only lads".

The principal officers were first mate, Michael Murphy, on a wage of eight pounds a month, Edward Kewley, the second mate, six pounds ten shillings a month and Hugh Cowan, the third mate earning five pounds a month. *Tayleur's* boatswain was paid five pounds ten shillings, the sailmaker five pounds and the ship's carpenter, six pounds six shillings a month.

Tayleur's master, twenty-nine year old John Noble of Whitehaven, was by all accounts, a courteous and cautious master-mariner of wide experience. Born in Penrith and orphaned at a young age, a ship had been Captain Noble's home since his early teenage years. Resolute and confident of his abilities, he had learned to take care of himself. Noble held a master's and an extra master's certificate. His examination board had been greatly impressed by his profound knowledge of maritime practice. Before taking command of the *Tayleur* Captain Noble had been the master of the clipper ship *Australia*.

When *Tayleur* was being built the owners, Moore and Company, approached

Captain Townson, the Chief Examiner of Masters and Mates of the port of Liverpool asking him to recommend an experienced and able captain for the Australia route. Captain Townson unhesitatingly put forward Captain Noble as "he was the most eligible man who could be selected to command the post". Noble relinquished command of *Australia* to accept the captaincy of Moore and Company's *Tayleur*.

When he was in command of the *Australia* Noble had taken emigrants to Melbourne and after landing his passengers there, he proceeded to Amoy in China from where he took a cargo to the West Indies. From the West Indies he returned to Liverpool. The round voyage had taken just over thirteen months and it was proclaimed to have been "one of the most memorable voyages on record". After this achievement the Company selected Noble to command their magnificent *Tayleur*. Without doubt John Noble was a seaman of great ability and certainly the right man to take command for the ship's maiden voyage.

Tayleur's passengers were gathered together from most European countries. There were 488 of them of whom 418 were counted as adult being over the age of 14 years. There were 56 children and 14 infants. The many foreign nationals contributed a veritable babble of languages. Just over half the passengers were English or Welsh – some of the latter could not speak English! From Ireland there were 111 emigrants with another 78 from Scotland. The remaining 39 were from Continental Europe or Scandinavia.

Irish emigrants leave home on their way to Dublin to embark for Liverpool.

Mid-Victorian propaganda encouraging the poor to emigrate to a better life in the colonies.

Emigrants awaiting medical inspection at the Emigration Commissioners office.

Very few of the voyagers were setting out solely for the adventure. It required a great deal of courage and moral strength to up roots to leave one's homeland forever but life in Britain had little to offer many of them. Most were escaping unemployment or starvation wages. The Irish left in tens of thousands fleeing periodic famine caused by the failure of the potato crop and some foreign passengers were leaving their homes to escape religious or racial persecution.

Although emigration was individual and largely unorganised, there were a number of philanthropic societies and trade associations which could help the intending emigrant. Assisted emigration was a way of building an empire and at the same time it reduced population as well as lessening the possibility of social unrest at home. But few of *Tayleur's* passengers seemed to have availed themselves of charitable assistance – they had sold everything they possessed to secure a passage to the land of opportunity.

Of the half million people who left Britain in the four years since the Californian Gold Rush of 1849 most were young labourers, servants, farm workers and unskilled factory hands. An observer who visited the ship just before she sailed stated, "The great majority (of the passengers) belonged to the farming, mining or artisan classes with only a very small number rating as clerks and they were mostly robust youths fit for any sort of work. There were some families numbering from four to five or six but few were of tender years."

It was a shabby, malodorous and confused assemblage of emigrants that clumped on board the *Tayleur*. The decks resounded to the pounding of hob nailed boots as groups of men, women and excited children lugged their boxes and bundles below deck to search for the spaces they were to occupy for the following couple of months.

Some of the steerage passengers were wearing all the clothes they possessed. Much of this was second-hand bought from old clothes stalls. In many cases it was obvious that coats had been crudely altered to fit new owners. The men's long, heavy greatcoats sometimes concealed two corduroy jackets and a couple of shirts. The majority wore woollen trousers or breeches with thick stockings and all had heavy boots. Tall ill-shaped felt hats were universally worn by the working man. The women favoured home-made dresses of cotton or coarse linen. Petticoats were made from stiffened material which held out the skirts. In most cases a bonnet was worn over a lace cap. Country girls preferred lace-up boots and every one possessed a knitted shawl.

The first class passengers had paid between £45 and £60 for their luxury berths. In the saloon they were provided with bedding, cutlery and tableware and they dined at the captain's table. The food was the best available with "livestock in liberal quantity provided throughout the voyage and the passenger is waited on as if in a hotel". The first class cabins were fitted with two berths. The second class cabins were also arranged with two berths and the passengers had the exclusive services of a steward. However, they had to provide their own bedding, cutlery and tableware. The fare in the second class was about twenty-five pounds. By shopping about between shipping companies an emigrant travelling in steerage could often obtain a passage for as little as £15.

The intermediate accommodation was advertised by the White Star Company as being "in the best part of between decks" and it was fitted with compartments of two and four berths. The space for the steerage passengers was divided into areas to contain four, six or eight emigrants and they could expect a daily menu which had been prescribed by Act of Parliament.

On the White Star ship the dietary scale for each adult passenger was printed and posted in the vessel. All passengers in second class, intermediate and steerage received a weekly allocation of one and a quarter pounds of beef, three and a half pounds of bread, one pound of oatmeal, six ounces of suet, two ounces of tea, one pound of sugar, a half pound of raisins, twenty-one quarts of water, six ounces of lime juice and a gill of pickles. In addition to the above rations, the second class passenger was entitled to half a pound of cheese. Cheese was not available to the other two classes. The second class emigrant also received more butter, preserved meat, potatoes, peas and coffee than the intermediate and steerage passenger. Children between one year and twelve years of age received half the adult ration. All passengers except those in the saloon accommodation had to equip themselves with a knife and fork, a spoon and a teaspoon, a tin plate and drinking can, a tin pint pot and a tin quart pot, a slop pail and a keg for holding water. All these items could be purchased as a kit in Liverpool for about one pound.

The shipping companies were bound by law to provide cooks to cater for the passengers. The ship's galley was situated on deck at the bows and food was carried below to be served to steerage passengers who were grouped into messes. Before the vessel sailed the emigration officer was required to make sure that the ship carried sufficient food, fuel, fresh water and cooking utensils for the voyage.

Strict rules were laid down concerning the amount and size of the luggage. The first class passenger could expect a storage capacity of about forty cubic feet for his luggage whilst the emigrant in steerage was restricted to fifteen cubic feet. Packages taken into the areas of accommodation were not to exceed two feet six inches in length, one foot eight inches in width or be more than one foot six inches in depth. The company recommended that all sea chests, trunks and packages should have the owner's names painted on them.

The White Star Company advised all passengers to report to the Company office immediately on their arrival at Liverpool. Here they could receive advice on everything from 'The Emigrant's duties and conduct in Liverpool' to 'Precautions to be observed on Arrival in Australia'. Above all, the passengers were warned of "a class of persons termed emigrant runners who force their services upon all who will accept the advice which they are most anxious to give. Advice from these men must be taken with great caution and indeed the emigrant will find himself better off by declining all communications with the class of men referred to".

Pilkington and Wilson advertised that their vessels always departed at noon on the stated departure dates. They claimed their ships were never delayed and that passengers could rely on them sailing punctually.

An 'Illustrated London News' depiction of emigrants relaxing between decks just after boarding at Liverpool.

There is no doubt that many of *Tayleur's* passengers had formed their conceptions of life aboard an emigrant ship from the many two-penny pamphlets available on the subject. There was advice in plenty and much of it was fatuous. In his booklet 'The Emigrant Voyages Manual', William Kingston listed a number of profitable ways of spending the long weary days at sea. He pointed out that beautiful objects could be made from meat bones saved from meals. Just as French prisoners of war had fashioned intricate models of ships during the Napoleonic War, so Kingston suggests the emigrant passenger could make sets of handles for dinner knives, they could carve animal heads for walking sticks and whip handles. Spoons and salt cellars made of bone would help the industrious to pass the time profitably!

Kingston urges passengers to try to keep fit by climbing ropes which had been fastened to the upper part of the main rigging and he advocates physical exercise suggesting that emigrants should seek out an old soldier who may be a passenger. "Be regularly drilled and learn platoon exercise. It give strength and grace to the figure." 'The Emigrants' Voyages Manual' advocates singing as a pleasant way of passing the time. "Thus are the angels employed. But let me urge you not to sing frivolous or indecent songs. If your companions commence any ribaldry stop them at once. Remember, on that very night a fearful storm may arise and you may be called into the presence of your maker." Not the most reassuring advice for the timorous voyager.

Kingston suggested emigrants make rag balls for deck games and he thought that they ought to be able to fashion boxing gloves. He approves of dancing and exercises with skipping ropes. Above all he urges the passenger to keep a journal and to enter the detail of the voyage every day.

Not all the passengers were in straitened circumstances for, according to a visitor to the ship, "Most passengers were emigrants of a superior class, a fact clearly indicated by the amount of gold known to have been in their possession after defraying all expenses here, namely £10,000. Shippers of goods also availed themselves of the great carrying capacity of the *Tayleur* and placed on board her a large general cargo valued at £20,000 making the total value of the ship and her cargo £50,000 independent of the specie in the possession of the emigrants raising the total amount to £60,000."

The ship had six classes of passenger accommodation. A few of the affluent were housed in the saloon and in the first class section. There was an intermediate category as well as second and third class compartments. The poorest of the emigrants were installed in steerage where conditions were spartan to say the least. On board ship the accommodation for the single men was to be found adjacent to the crew's quarters in the bows whilst the single women were allocated an area at the stern. The remaining large area of deck space was assigned to married couples and their families.

Most of *Tayleur*'s passengers had never seen a ship before they embarked and they were utterly perplexed by the situation on board. In spite of the recently introduced strict government regulations, conditions aboard many emigrant ships were appalling. Competition between the various companies had brought some improvement and there is no doubt that Pilkington and Wilson's claim that "*Tayleur* presents advantages superior to any ship hitherto dispatched to the Australian colonies" was largely true. Indeed, for comfort and safety she was unrivalled.

On the day before she was due to sail, government agents went aboard the ship to inspect the arrangements for berthing, ventilation and catering. The inspectors were satisfied. A visitor to the ship gave his opinion of the conditions on board. "Nothing could be more satisfactory in every respect. The first feature calculated to impress an observer was the ample room afforded for passengers in each compartment of the vessel owing to her large breadth and the excellent provision made for stowing away luggage leaving the tables and the space along the middle of the deck entirely unencumbered."

The passengers brought with them a mountain of luggage. Boxes and bundles of clothes, blankets and treasured family possessions. Some had been persuaded by newspaper advertisements to buy tents, patent lifebelts and waterproof clothing. Craftsmen heaved heavy boxes of tools aboard and although the ship's galley provided the food, many carried parcels of provisions. All this impedimenta had to be stored within a limited stowage space before the emigrants could settle into their living quarters.

The Embarkation. Emigrants board ship at Waterloo Dock, Liverpool in 1850.

Before the ship leaves port members of the crew search for stowaways. ('Illustrated London News') 1850.

Taking the roll call on the quarter deck just prior to sailing.

A romaticised painting showing emigrants grouped around a primrose - the last link with home.

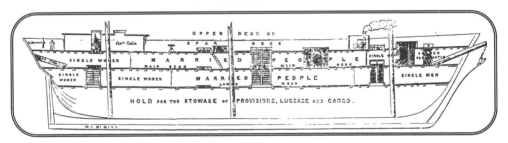

A comtemporary illustration showing a cross section of a typical emigrant ship of the 1850s.

With hundreds of passengers existing cheek by jowl for weeks on end the atmosphere in an emigrant ship's steerage accommodation was vile. The stench from unwashed bodies was all pervading especially in heavy weather when ventilation was restricted. However, in his inspection of the ship the unnamed visitor was most impressed by *Tayleur*'s system of ventilation. He said, "The ventilation was perfect throughout and it was obvious that in the event of stress of weather, the entire complement would be in the enjoyment of comfort below and the great difficulty experienced in many passenger ships of the space on deck not being left free for the working of the vessel could be avoided."

Government regulations demanded that every emigrant should submit to a medical examination. This was a travesty of an inspection for the doctor would simply glance at the families as they filed past him. So it was with the passengers boarding the *Tayleur*. The ship's doctor pronounced all fit with the exception of a woman and her daughter and the two unfortunate would-be emigrants were sent ashore. The year 1853 was one when cholera was rampant in Britain but, as the disease does not strike during the winter months, the ship's doctor had no anxieties that contagious illness would spread through the ship. He confidently predicted that he "Could keep the whole in perfect health throughout the voyage".

There can be no doubt that the passengers were relieved to be safely aboard the ship for Liverpool was no place for the uninformed and the gullible. The waterfront swarmed with lodging-house runners many of whom were street pirates who would cheat bemuddled emigrants and even snatch their luggage which they would return only after a ransom had been paid.

For a couple of days prior to boarding, some passengers had lodged in cramped attics and verminous cellars in Liverpool's slum districts. Most had suffered uncomfortable journeys burdened down with luggage but once aboard the ship they soon became confident and cheerful. It was warm between decks and this helped to promote feelings of optimism and contentment. There were no heart-rending decisions to be made, no more emotional farewells. Everything had been settled. The future would be a prosperous life in a country of unlimited opportunity. All were impatient for the voyage to begin.

On Saturday the 14th of January *Tayleur* was taken to her anchorage in the river and the following morning the Reverend James Buck of the Liverpool Seamen's Friend Society and Bethel Union went on board to conduct the Sunday service. Mr. Buck found that the ship "lay considerably up river" and he had an uncomfortable journey in wet weather before boarding her.

Mr. Buck was warmly welcomed on board by Captain and Mrs. Noble and by Mr. Wilson of the Company. Because of the rain, the service could not be held on deck so Mr. Wilson arranged for it to be conducted between decks. About two hundred and fifty passengers were then on board and they crowded around the minister who, standing on a box, called for divine blessing on the great undertaking on which they were about the embark. No one was forgotten in the blessing. Mr. Buck wrote, "We prayed for the divine blessing on the ship, the crew and their officers and commander and all the passengers whose temporary home she was to be for so long a voyage, not forgetting those who were left behind at home, or those who have preceded them in their departure from the land of their birth and were now upon the great sea."

James Buck was an experienced preacher. He had conducted countless services aboard emigrant ships and by the end of his address his congregation were so touched that he had their complete attention. Mr. Buck added, "Towards the close the still attentiveness which for some time had been growing, became pronounced and almost startling." After the closing hymn, the minister, assisted by Mr. Wilson, distributed leaflets that the Religious Tract Society had provided. The passengers then surrounded Mr. Buck warmly expressing their appreciation of his encouraging and uplifting address and he says that before leaving the ship his portfolio was filled with the addresses of families and friends left at home. He promised all the young people who had thrust addresses on him that he would send a printed account of the service and of his visit to *Tayleur* to their relatives and friends.

Mr. Buck, Captain and Mrs. Noble and Mr. Wilson and their guests then enjoyed some light refreshments in the saloon after which Mr. Wilson arranged for a small steamer to take the minister to the clipper *Indian Queen* on board which he was to conduct another service. The *Indian Queen* was another vessel chartered by Pilkington and Wilson. She was due to leave for Melbourne on the same day as *Tayleur* and the local press made much of the fact "the ships are competing and an interesting race is anticipated".

The next three days saw considerable activity to make the ship ready for her midday departure on the following Thursday. On Wednesday Lieutenant Prior, the first Assistant Emigration Commissioner for the Port of Liverpool went aboard to inspect the ship. It was his duty to see that the vessel was properly fitted out and that she was adequately manned.

The number of crew members required in a vessel chartered by the government Emigration Commissioners was four men for every hundred tons registered. By an old system of measurement which was still practised in the port of Liverpool *Tayleur* displaced 1,640 tons but by the new reckoning she was 1,979 tons.

Lieutenant Prior calculated the manning levels according to the old rules and he considered that three men for every hundred tons was sufficient for the working of the ship. He was certain that fifty-five seamen were a satisfactory complement. Lieutenant Prior declared, "The ship was in every way fitted out with crew, passengers and cargo. I never saw any ship better fitted." He added that the vessel had been constructed on scientific principles and that in every respect she was ready for sea.

But not everything was ready for the riggers were still working on the vessel a few hours before she was due to depart and the crew were engaged in tasks which should have been done days before.

Above:
Liverpool warehouses.
The Goree warehouses at
George's Dock.
Artist S.Austin.

Left:
Tall ships in Waterloo
Dock, Liverpool.
Artist W.G.Herdman

Among the last passengers to embark on the Wednesday was Robert Davison, a seaman from Kent, who was travelling steerage. Davison was an experienced mariner who had served twenty-six years at sea. He was surprised to note that the riggers had still not finished their work and he was concerned to see that new ropes were being fitted and that these had been stretched in cold weather. Davison said that if they had been stretched in warm weather the strands in the ropes would have tightened enabling them to run more easily through the blocks. He believed that the ship was undermanned but his first impressions of the crew were favourable and any misgivings he may have had he kept to himself.

John Aislabie, a passenger from Hull, also wondered at the riggers fitting new ropes. He said "The ropes had been put up dry and when wet they swelled, and even with major force they would not come through the blocks. The deck was covered with coils fresh from the manufacturers. We had riggers on board up to the moment of starting". Aislabie stated that in order to get the ship ready in time, the riggers worked all day on Sunday. He was definite in his view that " the ship was not fit to sail when she did, nor in all likelihood for a week longer".

Crowds of well-wishers cheer the emigrants as the vessel leaves the quayside.

Chapter Five: The Leaving of Liverpool

Thursday, the day of departure, dawned bright but cold. There was a flurry of activity aboard the ship as a late party of emigrants embarked. The preparations for departure and the changing scene on the river fully occupied the attention of the passengers. The Mersey was crowded with sailing vessels of every kind from full-rigged ships to tiny gigboats which were bobbing about conveying passengers, company agents and supplies to ships at anchor. There were coastal schooners, ketches, river flats, fishing smacks and steamers. The latter were hybrid vessels in that they carried full sets of sails. Long funnelled tugs fussed about, some towing trains of barges up river to the inland waterways. The passengers were fascinated by the various sights and the movement all around them.

Before an emigrant ship left port there was always considerable turmoil on board as a thorough search for stowaways was made. When all the passengers except those in first class accommodation had been assembled on deck for the roll-call, an officer and a number of the crew went below. Carrying masked lanterns and armed with long poles, the men poked into all the dark corners. Stowaways were often smuggled aboard ships in traveller's trunks and they were even found hidden in casks of ships' provisions so bed clothes were prodded, barrels inspected and boxes and chests were upended.

Just after mid-day there was considerable excitement among *Tayleur's* passengers as the paddle-tug *Victory* arrived to take the ship in tow. At last, at long last, the emigrants were on their way to a new life. On shore spectators raised their hats and waved their handkerchiefs. They cheered and the emigrants responded with a long, continuous shout of farewell. Orders were given, the tow rope was passed, the anchor raised and the *Victory* took the strain. Now there was no going back. The voyage had begun.

With a fair breeze from the south-east the ship began to slip past the docks and warehouses. The vast assembly of ships was described as "an immense multitude of vessels ensconced in the docks where the masts make an intricate forest for miles up and down the Liverpool shore". Some of the masts reached up over a hundred and fifty feet and in the rigging of some vessels there were dozens of seamen intensely interested in seeing the iron clipper making towards the open sea. *Tayleur's* very size attracted attention for the average Liverpool-owned ship of the day was no more than five to six hundred tons. The clipper was a Leviathan compared to the barques and brigs she passed along the waterfront.

The moment of departure. A crowded emigrant ship leaves the quayside in the 1860s. The illustration is taken from 'The Graphic'.

Under bare poles the ship was cheered out of sight. An observer noted, "So far as the passenger arrangements were concerned no vessel ever left this port with fairer prospects than *Tayleur* which was proved by the cheering on board as the vessel passed down river and the excellent spirits which prevailed. On deck everything was orderly and ship-shape. Her boats were all swung on the davits before she sailed and there was clear and ample space along her entire length for the operation of the crew. These were mustered, fifty or more in number, on the quarter-deck and afforded so fair a specimen of their class as could be desired. The officers appeared to be most active and intelligent men."

The great warehouses, the Custom House and the churches and public buildings of Liverpool began to recede as *Tayleur* passed the hulks of old men o'war which had been dismasted and roofed over to serve as quarantine stations or as accommodation vessels for retired seamen. Perch Rock Battery, the estuary fort at New Brighton came into view and then was quickly left astern.

Initially, the passengers were excited and elated but these emotions gradually gave way to feelings of quiet satisfaction. Then came a period of reflection followed by a solemn awareness of the occasion. As the sights and sounds of Liverpool faded, the emigrants took a long, last look at the land of their fathers, the country of their childhood, and a gentle sadness spread through the ship.

Under skies now grown overcast, the river fully justified Nathaniel Hawthorne's description. "The Mersey has the colour of a mud puddle and no atmospheric effect so far as I have seen ever gives it a more agreeable tinge." Certainly, there was no gleam of sunlight to cheer the scene as the passengers lined the rails to glimpse the last features of the shoreline. Soon *Tayleur* was out of the estuary and as the swells of the Irish Sea began to jolt the ship, the last of the afternoon twilight drained away and the shadow of the coastline disappeared. The deck quietened as most passengers retreated below. For the moment there was little to see.

In the short time they had been on board, the emigrants had begun to settle into the ship's routine. Every European language and every accent of the British Isles could be heard. Welsh quarrymen, Irish peasants, Yorkshire miners and pottery workers from Staffordshire rubbed shoulders with Danish fishermen and German dock porters. Servant girls from below the stairs of suburban villas packed in with Lancashire mill girls. In perpetual semi-darkness families occupied three-tier trough bunks, each family being separated from the neighbours by means of a board. Yet compared with the emigrant ships of the previous decade *Tayleur* was a comfortable and spacious vessel.

The competition between the shipping lines had proved to be of great benefit to both cabin and steerage passengers as their comfort was attended to in a manner unthought of in the days before the gold rush. Whilst the comfort of the cabin passengers was a priority consideration, the ship owners enforced strict rules to ensure the health and comfort of emigrants packed in steerage. Pilkington and Wilson promulgated ten company commandments which were posted throughout their ships.

The rules stated that all emigrant passengers unless sick, had to rise at 7am. Breakfast was from eight until nine o'clock but before then all bedding had to be rolled up and the decks had to be swept. The decks were also to be swept after every meal. Cooking fires were to be extinguished at 7pm unless required for the use of the sick. All emigrants had to be in their berths by ten o'clock and a safety lamp left burning all night. No naked light was allowed at any time or on any account. During the day if the weather permitted, the scuttles, stern ports and hatches were to be left open. All bedding had to be well shaken and aired on deck at least twice a week and no washing or drying of clothes was permitted between decks. Coppers and cooking utensils had to be cleaned each day. No passenger or member of the crew was allowed to sell spirits or strong drink to anyone during the voyage and smoking between decks was forbidden. Seamen were not allowed in the passengers' quarters unless on duty and no passengers were allowed to visit the fo'c'sle. Lastly, there was a reassuring decree forbidding any passenger from taking gunpowder on board ship.

The *Tayleur* was under tow for about sixty miles until six o'clock in the evening. She was then about seven miles north of the Skerries off Anglesey. The pilot in charge of the ship found that she behaved perfectly. He recalled, "She answered the helm and steered like a fish and I do not hesitate to say that she was the fastest ship afloat." During the passage the pilot examined the compasses and he found that there was a point difference between the compass on deck and those below. Apart from this he found no problems with the vessel.

It was now time for the *Victory* to slip her tow. The pilot, one or two company clerks as well as a number of friends of the passengers now prepared to board the tug to return to Liverpool. A breeze had sprung up and the tug was obliged to fall astern of *Tayleur* in order to avoid being run down by the ship.

The parting was a noisy business. When the tug came alongside the *Tayleur* there were shouts of command on both vessels and the intense activity of the crews and the clatter of the gear gave some passengers an impression of disorder. As soon as those returning to Liverpool were on board the tug, sails were hoisted on *Tayleur* and as the *Victory* turned away, the ship raced off at extraordinary speed.

As the *Tayleur* was speeding away the tug crew saw a man standing on the paddle-box. He was in some danger and was quickly pulled to safety. The man, an Irish emigrant, had panicked at the apparent confusion on board the ship and he had jumped onto the tug. He was very confused and demanded to know where the *Victory* was bound. When informed the tug was proceeding to Liverpool he became distressed and declared that he wanted to go to Melbourne. The tug master immediately put about in an attempt to catch the ship but although the tug reached her best speed of ten knots *Tayleur* was already making fourteen knots and there was no possibility of catching up with her. She proved true the popular maxim, "If a ship has Liverpool on her stern she is bound to go." *Tayleur* quickly disappeared into the darkness and the unlucky Irishman had to return to Liverpool whilst his luggage sailed off to Melbourne. The ship was not due to make a landfall until the coast of Australia came into view three months later.

A drawing of about 1850 shows emigrants at dinner in a spacious, well lit mess deck. Conditions were rarely as comfortable as those depicted here.

Chapter Six: The Maiden Voyage

From the very beginning things did not go well for *Tayleur*. Almost from the moment the tug disengaged the weather became boisterous and Captain Noble began to experience difficulty in handling the ship. There are many eye-witness accounts of early problems and all agree that the ship was very difficult to control. Indeed, some of the seamen and those passengers who were knowledgeable in maritime matters declared that because of serious design faults *Tayleur* was unmanageable.

The clipper was set on a disaster course from the instant she was released. Her maiden voyage was to be short. It was to last just forty-eight hours and the strongest vessel ever built was to come to an appalling end on a bleak coast a hundred miles from her port of departure.

The contemporary newspaper accounts of the voyage, the coroner's inquest and the official reports into the loss of the ship contain many references to the competency of the crew. A first class passenger, Mr. William Jones, of London who was described as "a highly intelligent and respectable gentleman" believed that the vessel was undermanned and that, "Because many of the crew could neither speak nor understand English, they were inadequate to handle the ship." Another passenger, John Abslaibie of Hull, said that he had plenty of opportunity of seeing the seamen at work and he was dismayed to observe that some foreign seamen were unable to understand their orders. He also believed that there were insufficient seamen to work the ship. Abslaibie was so alarmed that he approached the second mate stating his opinion that the vessel should return to Liverpool or seek shelter in another port. According to Abslaibie, the mate's reply was not reassuring, "If we put back to Liverpool or any other place every seaman on board will leave the ship." Abslaibie said that the mate indicated that he too, would leave the ship. The mate was alleged to have said, "There is such a scandalous crew on board that it is impossible to manage the ship in any way."

Another first class passenger stated that the first time orders were given to shorten sail he knew that the crew were, "Totally inadequate to manage the ship. The mate could not get anyone to go on the yards to shorten sail and the ship was at the mercy of the wind and the sea. Some idea of the incompetence of the crew may be formed when it is known that it took nearly three hours to take in the mizzen topsail and neither the maintopsail nor the lower sails could be got in at all. We, however, struggled through the night, our sails flapping and beating in a frightening manner. The boatswain and the third mate exerted themselves a great deal but the men did not appear to know their work. It immediately began to be whispered about that we would never reach the end of our voyage the crew being a mixed medley of many nations having an imperfect acquaintance with the English language and subsequently being unable to understand the captain's orders."

Mr. Robert Holland, gentleman, of Galway, declared that he knew something of nautical affairs and because he believed the ship was not properly handled he did not go to his bunk but stayed on deck in order to assist the crew. Holland said that both the mizzentopsail and the maintopsail were torn and he stated that, "I assisted, myself, in endeavouring to furl and clew up those sails as I saw that the men were not capable of doing it. I do not think there were enough hands on board. I mixed with the crew and I found that a number of them were foreigners. I spoke to them but they could not understand me nor I them. On Thursday night my apprehensions were so excited that I called some of my friends and urged them to come up to help. I considered that we were in great danger at the time."

Mr. Holland was one of a number of passengers who were to comment on the malfunctioning of the tackle. He said that the new ropes were stiff and he believed that the blocks were too small to allow them to run freely. He said that he saw a seaman go aloft to grease the ropes in order to lift the maintopsail. Holland declared that he heard the crew cursing the Liverpool riggers for sending them to sea in such a condition.

Robert Davison from Kent was to give evidence at an enquiry into the loss of the *Tayleur*. He was a seaman with twenty-six years experience and he was travelling as a passenger. Davison noticed that the vessel was being fitted with new ropes while she was in dock in Liverpool and he anticipated this would lead to difficulties. His fears were justified. He remained on deck throughout Friday helping to pull on the ropes and he found it a difficult task as they ran very hard through the blocks. When the wind increased he watched the crew reefing the mizzentopsail and he came to the view, "That the ship was not sufficiently manned but when the men had got accustomed to each other they would work her comfortably." Davison said that the ship was ready for sea, "Provided the people were used to the gear and everything was in its proper place but the crew were occupied in settling reef tackles which should have been done long before we left Liverpool." He also claimed that some crew had interpreters to translate the captain's orders.

A Mr. Michael Reidy of County Clare, gentleman, described the scene on deck on Friday morning. He asserted that he saw the greatest confusion, "I saw one of the sails torn and others flapping about without anyone taking care of them." There were very few sailors on deck so Reidy felt obliged to assist a couple of seamen who were hauling on a rope. Whilst he was engaged in the task the captain approached and spoke to one of the men who complained that they were short-handed because two of the crew were sleeping in the cradle. According to Reidy the captain stated that, "If he caught them sleeping they would recollect the time." Mr. Reidy took the opportunity to inform Captain Noble that, "The passengers felt greatly disappointed in the crew" and they were surprised that a commander of his character and experience should have put to sea with such hands. Noble replied, "I knew no more what they were than you did. They engaged themselves in Liverpool as good and efficient men and I had no opportunity of knowing what they were until now. I find that some of the fellows have gone down and hidden themselves in the passengers' berths." Reidy formed the opinion that, "The crew were very inefficient and that no person could be justified in thinking his life safe."

A member of the crew, seaman Joseph McLellan, gave his view of events. "I am a man before the mast. When we left the pilot, the wind came on very fresh and we were obliged to shorten sail, in fact she became unmanageable for the want of British seamen. We had only nineteen British seamen who could do their duty, the remainder of the crew were French, Chinese, Portuguese, Spaniards and I know not who. She answered the helm but became unmanageable as regards us reefing. Before the maintopsail could be managed it was split down to the close reef."

A second class passenger, Charles Lee of County Tipperary, said that he heard the captain give orders to reef the topsail but the crew were so inefficient that they took a considerable time to take in the reef. Lee was to allege that he heard Captain Noble tell passengers that if he had known the kind of crew he had he would not have put to sea with them. One first-class passenger was later to state, "The officers and the captain were attentive to the ship, although to me, there appeared to be some deficiency with regard to the crew. The captain himself said that out of the whole crew he could muster only fifteen sailors."

There were many passengers who were only too ready to lay the blame for the ship's erratic handling on the foreign members of the crew. Thomas Willet, a steerage passenger, said that he saw a seaman come down from the rigging and heard him say to the third mate, "If you have no better men to send up to assist me than those, I shall stay down and do no more for they can neither understand what I say, nor do they know their duty." The mate replied that he would send up more men and two seamen were sent aloft to help. A short time later the captain sent up the third mate to assess the situation. Willet alleged that when the mate returned he reported that, "There are three or four of those beggars lashed to the top asleep."

Without doubt, many of the passengers' accounts of events were unreliable and biased. Contradictory statements abound, some being patently absurd. John Rider a man of twenty-one declared that he, "Was accustomed to waterside pursuits." He thought that *Tayleur* was the most beautiful ship it was possible to imagine and all would have been well if she had been properly handled. He was certain that the crew consisted of, "Four Chinese, several Lascars and Danes with English boys who had not the least control over the ship. They were unable to hoist a sail without the help of the passengers." Rider was even more scathing of his fellow passengers whom he described as, "A rough lot, fit for any rascally deed."

Throughout Thursday night and the early hours of Friday the weather remained stormy. After the last sighting of the Skerries no observations were possible because of the hazy conditions. Shore lights were seen again on the following night. Captain Noble believed that this was the light on the Calf of Man whereas his third mate thought the vessel had returned to the Skerries light.

Tayleur was a brand-new vessel at sea without ever undergoing sea trials. Her sailing qualities were to be discovered on her maiden voyage and although the pilot found that "she steered like a fish" whilst under tow in smooth water, in heavy weather she proved to be unpredictable. Indeed, Captain Noble soon found that under certain combinations of sail the ship became unmanoeuvrable. At the height of the gale with a heavy sea running he was astonished to find that the ship would not obey the helm. He became convinced that his inability to wear the ship onto another tack by turning her head away from the wind was due to serious design faults. The captain was later to claim that the ship did not obey the helm because her foremast and probably the other two masts were set too far aft. He also suspected that *Tayleur*'s rudder was too small for such a large vessel. He found that the ship would not fall away from the wind and he was constantly frustrated by the sluggish response to the wheel. "She would not pay off. I could assign no cause for her not paying off but was much surprised by it. She answered the helm very badly. It took nearly an hour before she was turned on another tack and she drifted about five miles. Another vessel would have done this work in half the time and in only half the distance."

Every time Captain Noble attempted to manoeuvre the *Tayleur* the ship's wild gyrations made life an agony for the passengers. They were thrown about and shaken until they were too sea-sick to rise from their berths to get their meals. In the half-light between decks the despair, the curses and groans and the cries of the frightened children reduced the steerage to a veritable place of torment. The misery of the emigrants was such that many believed that they would die of sea-sickness before the voyage was half over. They did not care if they died. Death would be preferable to being tumbled about in a butterchurn for weeks on end.

Before long the seamen among the emigrants and those passengers who were seasoned travellers became apprehensive at the ship's antics and the rumour that the ship's rudder was too small began to gain credence.

An untried and perhaps inefficient crew, the stiff gear and the ship's refusal to obey the helm were major problems for Captain Noble but an even more serious situation developed. He became aware of considerable compass deviation. The first signs of variance between the compasses was noted by the pilot whilst the ship was under tow. The compasses had been fitted with compensating apparatus suitable for iron ships and yet within thirty hours the discrepancy between them was such that one showed a difference of two points, another one and a half points and the third also showed a large margin of error. On Friday night the third mate consulted the compass in front of the poop and found that it varied by a point and a half from the one aft. He could not estimate the ship's position. He said, "On Friday night we again saw the Skerries at about 9.30pm. I cannot say how it bore. I cannot say where we were in the interval. I cannot say where we ought to have been." Third mate Cowan was utterly confused. He had often sailed the Channel but he could not be certain that the light he observed on Friday night was the Skerries light which they had seen when parting with the tug twenty-four hours earlier.

The ship's officers frequently consulted the compasses but they received no comfort from the readings for the instruments did not agree. Captain Noble was certain that he was proceeding south down the centre of St. George's Channel whereas in fact *Tayleur* was heading due west towards the Irish coast.

Noble was navigating by intuition. The correct action was to have taken soundings. By using the lead and by consulting the Admiralty charts which indicated the various depths of the Channel, he would soon have realised that he was approaching danger. Soundings would have shown his position in almost the same way as milestones serve land travellers. Captain Noble did not take soundings to determine the ship's true position.

Mr. Badcock. a saloon passenger, had spent nine years at sea and he had therefore a professional interest in the workings of the ship. He believed that Captain Noble was a thorough master of his profession" but Mr Badcock was concerned at the variance between the compasses. He said that there were eight compasses on board and that no two appeared to correspond with each other at any time he examined them and he did so frequently. Furthermore, the ship's compasses did not agree with the pocket compasses possessed by passengers.

A Mr. William Thompson, the son of a Liverpool councillor, had decided to take passage in the *Tayleur* in preference to any other vessel because his brother had sailed with Captain Noble in the *Australia* and had spoken highly of him. Although the weather on Thursday night had been very stormy, Mr. Thompson thought that, "The ship behaved remarkably well and nothing occurred to cause the slightest anxiety among the passengers. Everyone appeared satisfied with the conduct of the captain and the officers." When conditions allowed, the ship made fast progress and reached a speed of nearly fourteen knots.

Thompson might have been pleased with *Tayleur's* early performance but Captain Noble was far from satisfied with her behaviour. As the gale increased Noble began to experience further difficulty in working the vessel and by the early hours of Friday he had become utterly frustrated by the ship's perverse conduct. She obstinately refused to turn onto another tack. Noble compared her unfavourably with his previous command. Under similar conditions *Australia* would have responded in half the time that *Tayleur* did and she would not have drifted for miles before doing so.

Some of the passengers were later to claim that throughout Thursday night the ship, "Had struggled through the night with her sails flapping and beating about in a frightening manner." They said that although the bosun and the third mate had exerted themselves tirelessly, the crew did not appear to know their work. Captain Noble was to refute this charge saying that when he required the mizzentopsail to be furled the reef tackle became entangled and the task required about twenty men and took about an hour and a half to complete. He said that because the operation was carried out in darkness it was understandable that a passenger who was not familiar with seamanship might believe that the situation aloft was not under control. In fact, he declared the topsail was eventually furled without too much difficulty.

A sailing ship captain led a remote and solitary existence. During severe weather or when the ship was approaching a hazardous coast or when the vessel was entering busy shipping lanes, the captain seldom delegated major responsibility. In these situations the master rarely left the deck but cat-napped throughout the night wedged into a sailcloth hammock-chair. Captain Noble remained on deck during the whole of *Tayleur's* maiden voyage.

Under storm canvas and with visibility reduced to a few dozen yards the ship beat about the Irish Channel for the whole of Friday making little progress because of contrary winds. During the morning the vessel was under close reefed topsails and maintopmast staysails but Noble again found that the ship would not pay off. He was carrying as much canvas as was safe for the conditions and because of the poor visibility he was unable to take observations. The ship's speed was reduced from eight to two knots when Noble left the deck for a few minutes leaving the first mate in charge of the ship.

The captain's brief absence allowed a number of second class passengers the opportunity of remonstrating with the mate pointing out the danger of keeping the ship so long on one tack. A seaman passenger said that he knew the Irish Channel and he stated emphatically that *Tayleur* must be near the Irish coast. He begged the mate not to keep the ship so long on the same tack. Before the mate could reply the captain returned. He was angry at the passenger's attempts to influence events and according to second class passenger Charles Lee, "Captain Noble said that he was the master of the ship and he would allow no man to interfere. The seaman hoped that he had not made any remark that was impertinent but as there were a great many passengers on board and as he was one of them, he had a duty to perform. Captain Noble made no remark but turned away."

The anxious passengers went below where they remained until daybreak. When they returned to the deck on Saturday morning they found that the ship was still sailing on the same tack. Once again the passengers attempted to argue with the captain but he refused to discuss matters and turned his back to them.

Under close reefed topsails, the ship's speed during Friday night rarely exceeded two knots an hour and in one ferocious squall seaman-passenger Robert Davison, thought that *Tayleur* would lose her masts. He said that when wearing, two men were required to take the wheel.

The accounts of *Tayleur's* last hours vary enormously and it is difficult to discern the truth. The survivors' reports of events are so diversified that they must be treated with suspicion. Some accounts are fallacious, others blatant attempts at self-glorification. Many are simply catalogues of blarney and egoism. Mr. Charles Lee was one of half a dozen passengers whose condemnation of the officers and crew must be open to doubt. His observations were naïve and much of his account of events was not supported by other witnesses. Lee's assertion that he had heard Captain Noble loudly denouncing his crew was a claim not corroborated by other passengers. However, it must be admitted that Lee was a man of considerable courage and his actions when the ship struck saved the lives of many passengers.

There were a number of passengers who claimed that they had helped the seamen to hoist sails. James Oldfield maintained that, "Some of the passengers who were sailors were got to work that night (Friday) as the crew were not able to do what was required." Oldfield also said that daylight found the vessel making little way but drifting to leeward. He said that, "The pumps were got to work as water was coming in rather fast." He also claimed that he knew that because of compass failure the ship's reckoning had been lost.

Able seaman Joseph McLellan was not a reliable witness. He held the opinion that at no time did Captain Noble know where he was. McLellan acknowledged that, "The captain was perfectly sober while on board but some of the hands were drunk (on Friday night). The three compasses did not agree within three points in consequence of the ship being iron. There should have been a compass at the royal masthead."

About six o'clock on Saturday morning the wind first changed to southward then it shifted to the southeast. The log was heaved several times between six o'clock and eight o'clock. The 'log' was a simple device for gauging the ship's speed. The apparatus consisted of a wooden float, which was cast overboard. Fastened to this was a line marked off at regular intervals that was attached to a reel on board. By counting the number of markings that the reel paid out in one minute, the officers were able to judge the *Tayleur's* speed to have been approximately five knots.

The vessel was heading south-west by west – at least it was according to the compass before the man at the wheel. The wind continued to increase and at eight o'clock single reef sails were set and the ship's speed increased to eight knots.

By nine o'clock a heavy gale was blowing and it became necessary to shorten sail.

Two hours later the ship was still on the same tack. Captain Noble later recalled the arrangement of sail that he had at the time. He said that by eleven o'clock the ship was under close reefed fore and mizzen topsail, double reefed maintopsail, foresail unreefed, foretopmast staysail and spanker.

It was about eleven o'clock when passenger Thomas Willet and a companion ventured on deck. Describing the weather conditions Willet said, "The waves were rolling mountains high and we were admiring the hills and valleys made in the water by the storm." As the two were thus engaged the weather suddenly worsened and all hands hastened to shorten sail. One of the crew recalled, "In the morning it was very boisterous and it blowed as if it would take the masts out of her."

Below deck a Mr. Nicholls of Devonport voiced his opinions on the handling of the vessel. He told his fellow passengers that the captain was wrong in carrying so much canvas as it would prove impossible to take in sail quickly if an emergency should arise. Rumours were rife and non-sensical theories proliferated. It was said that because the ship's boats on their davits offered considerable resistance to the wind this negated the movement of the rudder and made the vessel difficult to handle.

While sail was being taken in at about half past eleven the wind shifted in a sudden squall from the south-east. This dispersed the haze and just as the ship was paying off in response to the change in the wind, land was sighted.

At the look-out's cry of "Land-ho" Captain Noble ordered all hands to wear ship but although the crew acted quickly, *Tayleur* did not exert herself. She was slow to obey the helm, but in fifteen minutes she went off a point, arcing away from the danger so that Noble had no doubts that he could wear the ship to clear a dark coast that had suddenly appeared. He knew that the sails alone would not bring the ship round. He needed full assistance from the rudder. Under similar circumstances his previous ship would have cleared the coast easily but with '*Tayleur*' it would be a close-run thing. Nevertheless, the ship was making progress and undoubtedly, she would clear the cliffs of a bleak island which had appeared desperately close but then the wind changed and at the same instant there came the dreaded cry, "Breakers off the starboard bow" and the ship began to drive towards the rocks of Lambay Island at a terrifying speed.

Chapter Seven: The Cataclysm

The *Tayleur* was doomed. The passengers' recollections of the captain's actions at the fateful moment when land was sighted are inconsistent to say the least. One witness observed that Captain Noble was, "Quite steady and sober and dressed in a blue overcoat. I saw him occasionally looking out. At eleven o'clock I saw him looking intently over the starboard bow and a few minutes later I heard some of the crew say that land was in sight."

Passenger John Rider had a very different view of events. "I was on the deck before daylight and therefore saw all that happened. The man at the wheel saw land and reported it to the captain but he took no notice until he saw it himself when he seemed panic-struck and he ordered the ship to be wore but she was too close to the shore. I plainly saw that it was all over. Thank God I was perfectly calm as all depended on it. I threw off my coat. We were about a quarter of an hour from the time land was sighted until the ship struck. The crew were worse than women."

Another passenger alleged that after giving the crew orders to take in sail Captain Noble called the passengers to help him. He said, "If you want to preserve your lives you must come to these ropes and assist the seamen." Thomas Willet maintained that as the ship hastened towards Lambay Island every male passenger on deck helped the crew to take in sail by pulling on the ropes.

Lambay Island which was owned by Lord Talbot of Malahide is about five miles from the Irish mainland and thirteen miles north of Dublin. Its eastern coast is almost perpendicular with cliffs eighty feet high. At the base of the cliffs the depth of water is twelve fathoms in places. Nowhere along the length of the island's east coast is there a strand that would allow an attempt at beaching. The ship was being swept towards a precipitous rock face. The contemporary newspapers aptly described the coast as being a "Stygian shore" and certainly, it was a hellish place on that morning. Lambay had claimed ships before and it was the last place a captain would wish to be near in bad weather. In 1689 the 500-ton, 50-gun ship *Richard and Martha*, Captain Andrew Condore, went to pieces on the island and in the same year three small vessels laden with provisions for the Jacobite army were wrecked under the cliffs.

A couple of hours before danger appeared, Mr. Thompson, the Liverpool councillor's son, had a brief conversation with Captain Noble during which the captain said that after making little progress during the night because of adverse winds, the ship had begun to make better headway. Thompson was widely travelled and he was familiar with the routine aboard sailing vessels. Less than six months before embarking on *Tayleur* he had survived the destruction of the ship *Condor* which was burned at sea some eight hundred miles off the Brazilian coast. The ship was bound from Melbourne to London when by the spontaneous combustion of her cargo of wool, the vessel was burnt out. Just as the passengers had given themselves up for dead, a French ship arrived on the scene and took them off the wreck and landed them at Pernambuco.

Mr. Thompson was no stranger to danger and he was not alarmed by sounds of confusion on deck as *Tayleur* approached Lambay. The captain had told him that he intended to wear ship and Thompson assumed that this was the reason for the noise and he continued to read his newspaper. But soon there were cries of alarm, "We are going to be lost. We are on a lee shore." Passengers were running about the deck in frantic terror.

Thompson was about to go on deck when Dr. Cunningham, the ship's surgeon, hurried into the cabin. His expression confirmed Thompson's worst fears. The doctor gave no hope of avoiding catastrophe. "She is going ashore and a few minutes will decide our fates." Dr. Cunningham said that the ship was approaching a fearful rocky coast and that if the vessel struck there would be little chance of any being saved. He asked Thompson to go to the poop cabin to keep the ladies there as calm as possible. Thompson agreed and went to the poop cabin where he found the women becoming hysterical. He succeeded in keeping the women in ignorance of the true nature of events, "As that was the most desirable course to adopt in the circumstances." Dr. Cunningham then returned to the deck and Thompson never saw him again.

Whilst Thompson was endeavouring to reassure the ladies by giving evasive answers to their timorous questions another first-class passenger was alerted by a friend who came into his cabin and declared bluntly that the ship was about to go on the shore. "On deck a horrible scene of confusion met my eye. Before us at a short distance rose the bleak and rocky island of Lambay, round the base of which the waves were dashing furiously while the vessel, quite unmanageable in the hands of her crew, drifted towards it with fearful rapidity."

The horrified passengers could only watch as the captain and the first mate made every effort to wear the ship and when this proved to be impossible both anchors were released. The staysail was hauled down and the foresail hoisted in the hope of lessening the impact which appeared to be inevitable. The mate directed the man at the wheel to "keep her full" but the terrible drift to certain destruction continued.

Thompson, meanwhile was making every attempt to allay the fears of the ladies in the poop cabin. He knew that if the women went on deck they would add to the confusion and impede the crew in their attempts to manage the ship. In spite of the increasing disturbance Mr. Thompson managed to assuage the women's fears until the moment when the anchors were dropped. The thunderous vibration shook the ship from stem to stern and the women rushed from the cabin to join the terrified crowd surging on deck. The port anchor had been released first and after five hundred feet of cable had run out the ship was held momentarily but then the chain snapped and the starboard anchor was let go but its cable also broke when about five hundred feet of chain had run out. Neither cable had fouled in running out.

When all hope of getting clear of the island was lost Captain Noble ordered the sails to be set in such a manner as to bring the ship broadside on to the cliff so that the passengers would have a better chance to reach safety. As the ship was swept towards the shore Dr. Cunningham made desperate attempts to persuade the terrified passengers to keep out of the way of the crew so as to give the seamen room to work the ship. Survivors were to declare that, "Dr. Cunningham was seen everywhere trying to restore confidence and courage amongst the passengers and endeavouring to preserve order and coolness."

Most of those who survived the wreck of the *Tayleur* agree on the circumstances of her grounding. They said that the vessel approached the shore at an incredible speed. One moment she was hundreds of yards away from the rocks then in an instant she was lying below the cliff face. The ship rose on a back surge from the cliff and her stern came into violent contact with the rocks. The vessel was impaled with her stern about forty feet from the cliff and her bows less than twenty feet from the rocks.

The impact was so severe that at the stern the deck heaved up and buckled under the blow and at the same time there was the horrendous din of timbers being torn apart. The rudder began flailing against the rocks and became unshipped. On the next wave the vessel rose and was driven broadside against the shore. A wave swept over the deck amidships tearing everything loose and dislodging the boats. After two or three violent convulsions the vessel began to settle at the stern, the sea pushing the bows to within twelve feet of the rocks.

The noise was indescribable but the raging storm, the crashing breakers and the grinding of the ship's plates against the rocks did not stifle the agonising screams of hundreds of demented passengers. Captain Noble was roaring into his megaphone as he and his first mate urged the terror-crazed throng to keep clear of the masts in case they collapsed. Few of the passengers or crew could hear either of the officers.

The passengers had opened the stern ports so as to provide a means of escape. It was a vain hope for the water surged in to drown the sea-sick emigrants in their bunks. Another concussion smashed the *Tayleur* against the reefs and the stern began to sink trapping scores who were striving to reach the companionway. Terrified passengers struggled over the debris on deck, men carrying children, husbands dragging their wives. The survivors attempted to reach the bows but few succeeded. Most were swept overboard and drowned or they were dashed against the rocks and killed.

The scene was horrifying. Some were paralysed and were unable to make any exertions to save themselves but remained rooted to the spot. Women knelt on deck raising their arms to the sky calling for divine help. Some took leave of their friends, others perished when they went below to persuade their family members to come on deck. Two heavy seas, one immediately following the other swept away the poop cabin and the first class passengers who were sheltering there.

Seven boats were in readiness for lowering but when a passenger asked Captain Noble why he had not given orders to launch the boats, the captain despairingly waved his hand towards the huge breakers saying, "What is the use?". He did not give orders to launch the boats but nevertheless one was lowered only to be smashed to pieces under the cliff. A makeshift raft was rapidly assembled and some passengers used it to try to reach the rocks but they, like those in the boat, were thrown into the mill-race and drowned or they were hideously mutilated when they were hurled against the sharp rocks. Some young men jumped the gap but before they could get a foothold on the slimy rocks the breakers thundered in and swept them out to sea. A number did however succeed in reaching a narrow ledge safe from the scouring action of the waves.

One of the first to reach the shore was George Lewis, a miner from Merthyr Tydfil. Lewis fastened a rope in the rocks and at considerable risk to himself he assisted fifteen others ashore. In attempting to save one man, Lewis overreached and fell into the surf. Somehow he managed to regain a hold without letting go of the man whom he dragged to safety.

When the ship struck for the second time a black member of the crew, an assistant cook, managed to leap ashore with a rope which he secured in the rocks. Five or six more of the crew joined him and by this single rope and by means of a spar which the second mate used to bridge the gap a number of the passengers were got ashore. But the confusion and panic was so intense that coils of rope lying on the deck could not be reached because of the crowd trampling over them in the stampede to get to the spar. After a delay and with great difficulty, the ropes were pulled from under the feet of the screaming press of people and they were thrown ashore.

Husband's coaxed, pleaded and threatened their wives in order to get them to try to cross by one of the ropes. Some women did so, but between the ship and the shore their courage failed them or they were too exhausted to go on; they let go their hold to die in the pounding back wash, their death screams unnerving those who were preparing to follow. Some women had infants lashed to their backs. As they swung on the rope it sagged, their determination failed, fear gripped them so that they could not advance and they could not retreat because of those crowding behind. They were pushed off by those who were following and they, in their turn, fell in clusters as the ship staggered and keeled away from the rocks.

The scene was graphically described by James Oldfield who managed to cross to the rocks by means of the spar, "Numbers were stationed at the side of the vessel waiting for a chance to lay hold on the ropes which had been flung out – though many of those who did succeed in that object only the sooner met their deaths. It was one of the most agonising sights ever witnessed by mortal eye to see so many human beings especially women and children doomed to destruction almost within grasp of the shore.

Passengers crowd the rails as 'Tayleur' grounds on Lambay Island.

In a short time the vessel began to settle in the after part and the waves swept across the deck and carried upwards of a hundred wretched sufferers into the deep where they instantly perished."

One agile young passenger managed to swing ashore where he passed his rope to those on the rocks who held it taut so that a dozen other passengers were brought to safety. One of the fortunate few to escape down the rope was a Mr. G.T. Rimes, a cabin passenger who had spent most of the short voyage between decks attending to his wife and daughter who were seasick. When he heard the uproar as the ship approached Lambay, Rimes went on deck to find the vessel in imminent danger. He ran below and brought his wife and four-year old daughter on deck. When the vessel grounded Rimes slid down the rope holding his daughter by her clothing firmly clasped in his teeth. A second, married daughter followed him and the three were dragged to safety by a Mr. Ashley who had reached the rocks before them. Mr. Rimes never saw his wife again and his daughter's husband and her young child also died. Rimes' last memories of the ship were of the sea-sick passengers in their bunks, too ill to attempt to save themselves and oblivious to the desperate persuasion of family and friends.

A Mrs. Chasey was another of the few women to be saved. She was in her bunk when the ship struck. Her husband forced her and their young daughter to go down the rope. Sadly, Mr. Chasey and the girl did not survive.

As more ropes were flung ashore the ship began to stir and when the vessel lurched seawards the ropes were dragged from the hands of those ashore.

The situation on board the ship was now desperate in the extreme. "Wives were clinging to their husbands, children to their parents, women running wildly about the deck uttering the most heart-rending cries. Some offered all they had to any person who could get them ashore. One lady said that she had £3,000 in banknotes stitched into her stays. She offered £2,000 to anyone who could save her life – but in vain. She was drowned."

A group of young Irish women tried to cross on a rope. They got half way over and could go no further. For a moment they hung suspended over the maelstrom and then they were forced to relinquish their hold by others pressing from behind. None of the women succeeded in crossing the gap. All fell among the plunging wreckage between the ship and the rocks. Weighted down by their heavy voluminous clothing the women had no chance of survival.

One man forced his terrified wife onto a rope. When she could go no further and was dangling above certain death, her husband swung onto the rope and with his assistance the exhausted women was pulled to safety. But few were so fortunate. The ship's surgeon died hard. When his turn came to cross the rope, Dr. Cunningham had one of his children on his back and his baby held between his teeth. He had almost reached the outstretched hands of those ready to pull him to safety when the ship lurched, the rope tightened and the three fell into the sea. The children were swept away but the doctor managed to reach the rocks where he caught hold of a woman. He was pulling her ashore when a heavy sea swept them towards the ship. The woman drowned but Dr. Cunningham managed to seize a rope ladder which was hanging over the ship's side. He climbed back on board determined to rescue his wife who was in the midst of the frenzied mob which swarmed about the ropes. Within a minute he had found her and the couple embraced for the last time. As they were crossing a spar a great wave crashed over them and they were swept to their deaths.

Charles Lee estimated that twenty-five minutes after striking the rocks the stern to midships was under water. He said that in that time only thirty passengers had reached the shore, the majority by leaping onto the rocks. Lee and John Gibson, a passenger from Cavan, went to the bows where they found a spar which they forced across the gap. The two men crossed to the shore and stood by the spar to prevent it from being shaken off the rocks. Lee claimed that a hundred passengers crossed the temporary bridge to safety. The spar held for perhaps fifteen minutes until the ship gave a great heave and dragged it from the rock and all communication between ship and shore was lost.

For those who attempted to swim ashore there was the added menace of hurtling flotsam. Heavy wreckage was being propelled in and out by the breakers. Often the timbers were of little help to those who had seized hold of them for they were simply pounded against the rocks with added violence. Mr. Thomas Codd, a member of a well-known Dublin family had managed to swim to the shore. He was being pulled onto the rocks by another passenger when the two were swamped by a huge wave. When next seen the men were far out to sea and beyond help.

Edward Tew, a banker's son from Wakefield, was so horrified at the sight of the mass of corpses tumbling about between the ship and the shore that he decided to swim to seaward in the hope of being washed ashore at a safer place. He dropped down a chain into the sea where he saw a boy about ten years of age clinging onto a piece of wood. The boy was crying. He said that he had seen his mother drown and that it was no use Tew trying to rescue him for both were about to die. Tew grabbed the boy by his collar and pulled him onto a large spar. He kept hold of the boy whilst trying to fend off floating debris. His description of his rescue attempt is harrowing. "I experienced difficulties which required superhuman efforts to overcome. A heavy sea was rolling over us and almost perpendicular rocks as black as death staring us in the face. I determined not to have our heads dashed against the rocks as had been the fate of so many of our fellow passengers. As we neared the rocks the boy was washed off the spar but still I had hold of him. I put out my hand to save our heads and received a cut on my hand but I felt the land and I told the boy that we were saved. But not so, for we were washed back again. I made to land a second time and was washed back again. I tried a third time and was treated in the same way. I was making towards the rock a fourth time determined to save the lad or die with him when a spar struck him on the side of his head and entered his skull. It knocked me under at the same time but I rose again and a rope was thrown to me which I twisted round my arms twenty times and with the assistance of a sailor I clambered up the rock. I got there just in time to see the whole ship go down."

The final moments before the ship sank were vividly described by a survivor who believed that he was one of the last to be rescued. "The scene was now most truly awful. The most desperate struggles for life were made by the wretched passengers. Great numbers of women jumped overboard in the vain hope of reaching the land and the ropes were crowded with hundreds, who in their eagerness and terror and confusion frustrated each other's efforts for self-preservation. Two men came ashore with children tied on their backs but of the whole who fell into the sea not above five were saved."

The boatswain, William Sheardon, made strenuous efforts to get the passengers off the sinking ship. One of the last to leave, Sheardon went along the spritsail yard and fastened a rope to it then, helped by others on the shore, the bosun encouraged passengers to climb onto the yard and swing clear of the ship. However, there were others of the crew who did not acquit themselves with credit. Some survivors were to allege that the Chinese and Lascars made no attempt to help in the rescue. "As soon as they had succeeded in making good their landing they scampered with all haste up the rocks never attempting to assist those left on board." The correspondent of the newspaper *Morning Herald* on the other hand, reported on the gallantry of two foreign members of the crew who rescued a two-year old child at considerable risk to their own lives. Another seaman, Patrick Bailey, described as "a fine specimen of a sailor", had his arm broken in his persistent attempts to save a woman.

As the stern began to sink the vessel lurched so that the ropes, spars and studding-sail booms were pulled away from the rocks. With the last connections to the shore now severed, the panic-stricken passengers rushed towards the bows but, as the ship sank lower, the seas scythed across the deck, each wave taking scores at a time. They could be seen struggling in the surf for a moment or two and then they were gone – swept away in the undertow.

One young woman fell from a rope but managed to get hold of another which was hanging from the side of the ship and which she held on to for a quarter of an hour. Time and time again she was smashed against the side of the vessel but nothing could be done to save her and after a brave struggle she disappeared. Most of the women were too terrified to venture down a rope although at first the risk was not too great but, when the vessel began to settle, the chances of escape were considerably reduced. One survivor noted grimly, "All the weak and helpless were lost and nobody who could not make an effort was saved."

It was still possible for the more courageous and athletic young men to jump to safety from the bows onto the jagged rocks but as the vessel edged away from the shore few managed to clear the terrible gap. They fell into the breakers and were battered to death against the rocks.

In the last few moments of the ship's life there were many heroic actions. Just before the hull went below the surf one man saved his wife and son. The father commanded his twelve-year old boy to jump to the shore. The boy did so and the sight of the lad standing on the rocks with his arms outstretched beseeching his mother to jump gave her the courage to hurl herself ashore. The father followed and the three were pulled to safety.

Once on the rocks the shocked and injured survivors were faced with a climb up a precipitous and slippery cliff face with narrow ledges for footholds. For many, the eighty foot ascent was an impossibility but seamen used ropes to pull passengers up to the top and in the bitter east wind throughout the dark winter afternoon, the survivors were hauled clear of danger.

Passenger Edward Tew, the second mate, Edward Kewley and Captain Noble were the last to leave the stricken vessel. The captain had stripped to his shirt and trousers. He was up to his waist in water on the bowsprit when he jumped. As the hull was disappearing below the water he swam the few yards to the rocks. As he did so he could feel the drowned passengers below the surface. Encouraged by members of his crew urging him on from the shore, the captain managed to reach the rocks. He was pulled to safety by a young man but just as Noble had secured a hold on the rock, a sea carried away his young rescuer. The second mate who had stayed with his captain to the end never reached the shore alive. His body was washed onto the rocks.

A survivor from Winchester said that the sinking of the ship was not sudden but that she settled gradually before moving off the rocks to remain stationary with most of her rigging above the water. There were many passengers still on board and as the vessel slipped into deep water, they crowded into the bows. Very few of them survived. The witness described Captain Noble's last moments on board his command. "Amongst those on the bowsprit was the captain who had divested himself of all his apparel except his shirt. Several of the crew who had gained the rocks called out to him to jump into the sea and swim for it which he did by means of a rope which was thrown to him. He gained land safely. He was the last man to leave the ship as the hull was disappearing below the water."

There were many accounts of the final minutes when the passengers had crowded towards the bows. One brief report will suffice to illustrate the horror of the ship's last convulsion. "Those who attempted to escape from the bows all, or nearly all of them lost their lives. The moment they fell into the water the waves caught them and dashed them violently against the rocks and the observers could see the unfortunate creatures with their heads cut open, struggling in the waves before sinking below."

In newspaper interviews Edward Tew spoke highly of Captain Noble's conduct throughout the disaster. He said, "The captain's conduct during the whole melancholy scene was most praiseworthy. I never saw him take a drop of liquor and from the time of leaving port he was never in bed nor did he obtain the slightest rest."

Individual members of *Tayleur's* crew were later praised by survivors who said that some seamen had shown courage in getting them off the ship whilst other crew members had pulled passengers ashore at some risk to themselves. It was pointed out however, that the crew had been first to leave the ship and surprisingly few of them had been lost. It was also reported that when the ship struck discipline among the crew had broken down completely. It was said that unable to make himself heard above the storm, Captain Noble attempted to regain control by striking the seamen with his megaphone. One passenger praised the captain but had little good to say about the crew. "In my opinion the crew was not sufficient for such a large ship. The crew were the first to abandon ship."

Tayleur had gone. It had taken about twenty-five minutes from the time she struck the rocks until the hull disappeared completely. In the final moments some passengers attempted to climb to safety in the rigging but they had left it too late and the seas plucked them off the shrouds and flung them into the swirling vortex of wreckage and bodies at the foot of the cliff. Only two men managed to climb above the cataclysm. When the whole length of the ship went below the water there was a fearful struggle from screaming passengers then all except the two men in the rigging were gone.

The ship's masts remained above the water and for hours after she had sunk the two men could be seen waving their arms in order to attract the attention of those on shore. Nothing could be done to rescue them for those on the shore were in no condition to help. Then it was noticed that a back surge from the cliff was carrying wreckage back towards the ship. Ropes were fastened to the ends of a large piece of timber which was floated out to the vessel and by this means one of the men was pulled to safety.

The other man, William Vivers of Dumfries, remained lashed to the rigging in the biting wind for fourteen hours. The survivors on shore could see his frantic waving but they were too exhausted and shocked to devise a way to help him. Vivers vigorously exercised his arms and legs to keep himself warm. When he saw the survivors leaving the shore he came near to despair. An hour later he was to witness a gruesome sight when the *Tayleur* shifted. As the ship moved, the bodies of the trapped passengers surfaced. It was like the day of judgement for, it was reported, "The bodies of the dead rose again and scores were visible in all directions. Husbands, wives and children clasped in each other's arms and he saw several mothers whose last convulsive grasp was still rigid around the lifeless limbs of their children."

With the gale howling through the rigging and torn canvas, Vivers lapsed in and out of consciousness. When he came to, he resumed his exercises but then, overcome by fatigue, he fell into a deep sleep. In the meantime some survivors had reached the coastguard's cottage on the other side of the island.

As soon as Mr. Finlay, Lambay's coastguard, heard of the wreck he and a number of survivors went to the scene. After a great deal of shouting they managed to wake Vivers who was by this time "in an exhausted and almost lifeless condition". About two o'clock in the morning in a lull in the storm the coastguard managed to get a rope around Vivers and with help from the survivors he was pulled from the rigging. He was carried to the coastguard's cottage where, "Mrs. Finlay left her bed and treated him in the most humane manner. You may fancy the poor fellow's joy at his deliverance."

A contemporary engraving graphically captures the Tayleur's final moments.

Chapter Eight: Lambay. "A Stygian Shore"

In order to reach the top of the cliff the exhausted survivors had to climb an almost vertical rock face. Using ropes, the uninjured helped the timid and those with sprained or broken limbs to scale the cliff by moving from one narrow ledge to the next. Most climbed without shoes or stockings. Captain Noble suffered cuts and abrasions. He had lost his trousers in coming ashore and was wearing only his shirt. Many survivors were half naked having taken off their clothing before leaving the ship.

Suffering from cold, shock and injury and soaked to the skin in the teeth of a pitiless biting wind the wretched mass of survivors assembled on the cliff top. Here desperate husbands searched in vain for their wives and children, crying out in anguish when they realised their families had perished. Harrowing displays of grief and despair were to continue through the night and for days afterwards. As there was no shelter of any kind on the cliff top, the men closed ranks in an attempt to provide a windbreak around the few women and children who had survived the wreck. One or two members of the crew went to find help whilst a host of two hundred disconsolate and grief-stricken victims moved off to seek shelter.

The nearest source of aid was two miles away on the other side of the island. There were a couple of coastguard cottages but only one substantial building. This was a house, or castle, that was the summer residence of Lord Talbot de Malahide, the owner of the island. As soon as he saw the survivors Lord Talbot's steward opened the house to them. Straw was carried from the barns and strewn over the floors to provide bedding, a pig was killed and bread, potatoes, biscuits and whiskey were made available.

The coastguard received his first intimation of the disaster when he was confronted by a group of tattered and forlorn figures who appeared on his doorstep. He took in as many people as his cottage would hold and arranged for others to be accommodated in a couple of adjoining dwellings.

The kindness of the Lambay folk was said to have been "beyond praise". The survivors were unanimous in their appreciation of the benevolence of the islanders who did everything possible for their relief. Every morsel of food the islanders possessed was divided among the injured and what little they had in the way of clothes, footwear and bedding was willingly given. In the week following the wreck the islanders and the coastguards recovered some of the passengers' personal effects from the scene of the tragedy. Every item found was listed and surrendered to the authorities on the mainland.

Over two hundred and eighty of *Tayleur's* passengers and crew had reached safety. Even in the aftermath of such an appalling catastrophe the class system continued to operate. The Dublin newspapers later reported that; "Several of the more respectable class of passengers had obtained shelter in the coastguard station or in the few cottages adjoining whilst the great mass of people rescued had bivouacked in a grassy hollow under the shelter of a hill, their encampment being fortified with boxes, packages, parcels, sea chests and bedding. All were found to be suffering many privations."

The death-toll was horrifying. Entire families had been annihilated. One man, Alexander Ball, lost thirteen members of his family, he alone survived. All nine members of the Boar family died, all nine members of the Jaffray family were drowned. The father, mother and the six children of the Ross family perished. All six of the Postlethwaite family, the six Hendersons, six Stanlakes and the five members of the McKenzie family died. John Harper lost his wife and his five children. An unnamed man was reported to have lost his wife and his five children, his brother, his brother's wife and her three sisters. A German emigrant was the only survivor of a family of six.

Two hundred and ninety-one, well over half of *Tayleur's* passengers died. Only six members of the crew were lost including the second officer and three of the young apprentices. So the death-toll was two hundred and ninety-seven. Unconfirmed reports stated that there were five unnamed stowaways on board and that they all drowned.

Of the hundred women on board only three survived. Four children aged from one to fourteen years were rescued out of a total of fifty-six. One infant, of less than twelve months old, lived out of the fourteen babies carried aboard.

The status of the passengers rescued was variously reported but in one respect the accounts agree. Of the sixteen first-class passengers accommodated in the luxury deck saloon only one managed to reach the shore. About sixty steerage passengers and ten travelling third class reached safety as did fifty-five intermediate and thirty-seven emigrants who had travelled second class. Although only one first class passenger from the saloon was saved, the number of first class passengers in cabin accommodation who managed to get to safety was remarkable. Thirty-seven of them lived.

Throughout the night the gale continued to tear across Lambay. Semi-naked, wet through and pinched with hunger the survivors suffered agonies. In the opinion of the coastguards the heavy seas made it impossible for them to cross to the mainland. Nevertheless, at daybreak on the Sunday morning a boat was launched and crewed by men of the island and a survivor, Thomas Kemp, it reached the mainland to bring the first news of the wreck.

Kemp was a courageous individual. When the *Tayleur* sank he had escaped death by a hairsbreadth. Falling from the bowsprit, he was rescued by a man who managed to catch him by his trousers as he was being swept out to sea. Yet within hours of being rescued Kemp was risking his life by crossing to the mainland in a tiny scallop of a boat.

Once ashore Kemp reported the news of the disaster to local dignitary, Sir Roger Palmer, in the village of Rush. Palmer immediately hired a fishing smack which, with a volunteer crew, crossed to Lambay with four carcasses of mutton, bread, oatmeal and thirteen gallons of whiskey. Kemp also contacted Mr. Walsh, Lloyd's agent in Dublin who hurried off to make arrangements for a steamer to proceed to the island.

If anything the gale increased in severity on Sunday and although it was probably a foolhardy mission, a party of coastguards from Rush set out and crossed to the island with supplies for the survivors.

When Dr. Speering of Rush heard that there were injured among the crew and passengers of the *Tayleur* he insisted on making an attempt to cross to Lambay but heavy seas forced the boat to return to harbour. Lieutenant Senior R.N., the officer commanding the coastguard station at Rush, also crossed to the island taking bread, tea, coffee and sugar. The weather was atrocious and Senior described his return journey as being difficult and dangerous. A few hours later the storm abated and the coastguard boats made trips taking food to the island and bringing off a number of survivors who, on arrival at Malahide, were sent to Dublin by train. The improvement in the weather was short-lived for the gale returned with added ferocity and once again the island was cut off from help from the mainland.

For those on Lambay who were in the open without shelter from the icy wind and rain, the first night proved almost as great an ordeal as their escape from the ship. They had lost all they possessed. The following is typical of the statements made by survivors and which were reported in the newspapers during the following week. "The night was dreadful and we were almost starving from hunger. Many of us were nearly naked. The next day was worse than the day before. Most of those who had succeeded in getting ashore lost all their earthly possessions except the clothes they wore and several had thrown off their dress before leaving the ship. I had sold everything to pay for the passage and outfit. That is all lost with the vessel and I have neither money nor clothes nor have I any situation or work." Another survivor told of the scale of losses incurred by one of the better-off passengers. "The loss of property was immense and no one seems to have been insured. One man said that he had lost goods to the value of £750."

Very few of the *Tayleur's* passengers were able to salvage anything of their personal property but there was one notable exception. The *Manchester Guardian* reported how one astonished survivor's goods were restored to him, "A young man was sitting with us in one of the coastguard cottages getting some thick porridge when two girls came into the cottage carrying a chest which they had found on the shore. The young man instantly said that it was his although the water and rocks had stripped it of its cloth covering. He said the chest contained all his clothes and money and taking his keys from his pocket, he at once unlocked it and raising a shirt or two immediately drew forth the sum of £50 from which he gave the girls who had saved the trunk a sovereign each."

One of the survivors was a Samuel Carley who was returning to Australia. In 1841 Carley was sentenced at the Rutland Assizes to ten years in Botany Bay "for sheep slaughtering". At the time he was about to marry Sarah Ann who was pregnant with his child. She was present in court during the trial and was confident that he would be acquitted. When the sentence was passed she threw herself around the prisoner's neck overcome with grief. Carley was banished to Australia and Sarah Ann was forced to seek work making corsets to provide for herself and her child – the paternity of which the prisoner did not deny.

Twelve years passed without the woman receiving news. Then one day on a railway journey to Stamford she was seated in a compartment in which there were several men, one of whom stared at her intently. In order to escape his apparent rudeness she changed seats. As she did so the man caught her eye and jumping to his feet exclaimed, "I am the man." Sarah Ann recognised the voice of the long lost Samuel Carley and after fainting gave expressions of great joy. A few days later the couple were married and Carley who, after his release from the penal settlement, had been a successful gold digger, persuaded his wife to accompany him to Australia where, he was sure, he would be equally successful in a second gold prospecting venture. They were steerage passengers on board *Tayleur*.

Samuel Carley managed to rescue his wife and his twelve-year old son, Robert. We know nothing of Carley's subsequent history for there was no follow-up newspaper story and the family disappeared from the public-eye. But then, that is probably what Samuel would have wanted. However, the story of Samuel Carley was widely reported in the national press and it has some similarity to the adventures of the fictional Abel Magwitch in Charles Dickens' novel *Great Expectations*. Perhaps Samuel Carley was the inspiration for Dickens' famous convict?

The youngest survivor was an unknown baby boy about twelve months old who was said to have been rescued by a French passenger who brought the child ashore by carrying him in his clenched teeth. The child's parents were thought to have been among fifty emigrants who were swept away by a large sea as they struggled to reach the bows of the sinking ship. When the wave receded the child was seen lying on deck from where he was snatched to safety by the passenger.

As the weather worsened on Sunday many survivors began to despair of imminent deliverance from their sufferings. Few were prepared to venture into the gale to the site of the wreck. However, as soon as it was daylight one sturdy passenger returned to the cliff top from where he helped to recover the bodies of some of the dead. The young man helped a number of the seamen to descend the cliff face. He braced himself in a crevice and wrapping a rope around his waist, he lowered the men down to the rocks. In order to keep him warm other survivors pulled up the turf and wrapped it around his body. The man refused to accept help and for an hour he continued to haul bodies to the top of the cliff. He was determined to continue his work of compassion because he explained, "I was obliged to remain with my foot wedged against the rock and in this way I could have supported a bullock." The charitable young man was one of a number of passengers who were to cry out against the inhuman treatment of the dead who were stripped of their valuables. "There was only one lady brought up the cliff. She was naked all but her stays and she had two diamond rings on her fingers. I was told that about two hours after some inhuman monster had cut off her fingers for the rings."

Daylight revealed the full horror of the tragedy. About sixty bodies were tumbling about in the surf. The corpses were naked, the sea and the rocks having torn away their clothing. Some of the victims had been flung high up the rocks and lay caught in fissures above the waves. Most of the victims, "Had been mangled in such a way by being dashed against the rocks that no one could tell who they were."

The hull of the *Tayleur* was completely submerged but her masts with three reefed topsails were upright and still intact. The ship had come ashore between a promontory known as "The Nose" and an inlet called the "Seal Hole". On a narrow strip of shingle at the foot of the cliff there was a mass of piled wreckage, bedding, clothing and mutilated corpses.

One man watched the crew members and the coastguards as they recovered the bodies from the rocks. "We went out to see the wreck and found the bodies piled over one another. It was enough to make the stoutest heart shudder. One poor female was lying on the ground naked. In this state she was left. Several persons were getting all they could from the bodies. The coastguard said that the men who saved the things had a right to them. Captain Noble said that he would have nothing to do with it. God grant that we may never witness such a scene again."

As the gale continued, the survivors on Lambay saw that immediate help from the mainland would not be forthcoming. Most were anxious to inform their relatives that they were safe. One tactless individual was prepared to pay a large sum of money for conveyance to the mainland. "Throughout the day I offered anything if they would put me across to Rush as I wished to telegraph home that we were safe before the news of the wreck arrived but for some reason they appeared to wish us to stay in this wretched state."

On hearing the news of the wreck, Mr. Walsh, Lloyd's Dublin agent, hurried to the offices of the Dublin Steam Packet Company whose secretary readily agreed to put the steamer *Roscommon* at his disposal. Unfortunately, *Roscommon* could not quickly be made ready for sea as "she had blown off her steam" so the steamer *Prince* commanded by Captain Dearl, was prepared for the work of rescue. However, many of the *Prince's* crew including her engineers were ashore for the weekend and they could not be located. Luckily Mr. Donaldson, the chief engineer of the *Roscommon* and his assistant were available and they were eager to act as engineers on the *Prince*. A motley crew from both steamers then set out for Lambay. Fortunately, Captain Dearl was able to obtain the services of a Mr Kearns who was 'a branch pilot and a man of skill and experience as regards the soundings off Lambay".

By the time the *Prince* had arrived off Lambay darkness had fallen and because a heavy sea was still running it was too dangerous to lower the boats to go to the island. The steamer anchored in the lee of the island about half a mile from the shore. Captain Dearl ordered that the boiler fires were to be constantly stoked so that he could get steam at ten minutes notice.

On Lambay the survivors' spirits soared at the news that a steamer had appeared off the island but when the gale continued unabated and it became obvious that the vessel had anchored for the night the survivors became downcast. The thought of another night on Lambay depressed even the most indomitable.

At daybreak on Monday *Prince* steamed within a cable's length of the island and as her three boats approached the shore, the survivors came streaming down to the landing place. "The aspect of the sufferers was deplorable in the extreme. All were suffering from cold, terror and exhaustion whilst many had their limbs and heads bound up having received injuries, bruises and wounds more or less severe by collision with the rocks. Too much praise cannot be given to Captain Dearl for his prompt measures in bringing the passengers from their forlorn and cheerless situation and also for the care and kindness with which he ministered to them on board."

On arrival at the *Prince,* each boat of men, women and children were divided into messes in the after steerage where coffee and hot soup was provided for them. Many of the injured had to be carried on board.

Whilst the boats were ferrying survivors to the *Prince* a number of the steamer's crew together with Mr. Walsh and Mr. Allen of the Dublin Steam Packet Company and others including newspaper reporters set out to cross the island to the wreck. They found that heavy seas almost mast high were sweeping over the ship and that she was starting to break up. The men reported that, "The foremast, foretopmast and stump of the foregallant mast were still standing, the main and mizzen topmasts had been carried away, the foretopsail remained still set and was split in the centre. The ship appeared to be aground at the bows but hung in deep water at the stern. Immediately under the bows in a narrow creek where the force of the tide converged, the strip of sand and shingle where the shore is very steep, was found literally covered with dead bodies both male and female, the remains of the unhappy creatures who had endeavoured to save their lives by letting themselves down by bow ropes or the bowsprit rigging but who were washed from their hold by the force of the waves. Along the strand on either side of the creek the shore was strewn with dead bodies, boxes, packages and sea chests."

Because of the rough seas no attempts could be made to recover the dead or to salvage objects from the wreck. The dejected party then returned to the landing place and to the *Prince.*

When about two hundred and thirty survivors had been taken aboard the *Prince,* Captain Dearl gave orders for the steamer to proceed at full speed for Dublin where she arrived at the North Wall at 2pm. Captain Noble and twenty-five of his crew remained on the island in order to salvage and secure what could be removed from the wreck.

Without doubt, the most distinguished survivor was the child who was believed to have been rescued by the French passenger. On the short journey to Dublin practically everyone on board the *Prince* had filed through the saloon to see the little orphan of the storm. The following day the *Evening Mail* published a letter from the Reverend T.H. Armstrong who stated that he had seen the child, "Who was saved, some say by a wave which swept away fifty human beings leaving him unhurt among the rocks. Others say that he was rescued by a Frenchman who carried him from the wreck in his teeth." Mr. Armstrong visited the *Prince* and found the child in the care of the steamer's steward and stewardess. He offered to take it while the two were away for a week on a voyage to Liverpool. Mr. Armstrong took the child and began an appeal for funds for the boy's future support.

On arrival at Dublin the pitiful crowd of survivors was taken to the Steam Packet Company's office where they were each given five shillings for their immediate needs from funds subscribed by the Dublin Chamber of Commerce and a number of them also received tickets for lodgings in the city. The majority were accommodated in a warehouse which was made available by the Waterford Steam Packet Company. Here, many Dublin folk pressed forward seeking news of their relatives who had been on board *Tayleur*. Sadly, it was reported that, "Almost everyone enquired for was lost."

About thirty passengers required hospital treatment mainly for broken bones and severe lacerations. They were visited by Mr. Walsh who kept them informed of the charitable efforts that were being made on their behalf.

Some Irish survivors who, a few days earlier had set off for Liverpool in the best of spirits to emigrate to a new life, now abandoned the idea of seeking gold and happiness in Australia. Numbed by their experience, despondent and mourning the loss of their loved ones, the former emigrants refused the White Star Line's offer of a free passage to Liverpool and they set out to return to their home towns and villages. They had suffered enough. The sea would not have another chance to claim them.

On Wednesday the gale reached a crescendo. A storm of intense ferocity pounded the Irish coast. There was no possibility of communication with Lambay and the hardiest Malahide fishermen would not venture to cross the couple of miles of tempestuous sea. Mr. Ralph Cusack J.P., the agent to Lord Talbot de Malahide and some relatives and friends of the drowned passengers, had contributed a large reward which was offered to any boatman who would bring bodies from Lambay so that the inquest could take place. Many relatives wished to cross to the island in the hope of being able to identify family members but there was no let up in the weather and the reward attracted no takers. The grieving relatives were forced to return to Dublin but they were heartened at the news that Lord Talbot de Malahide had offered to place his private yacht at their disposal when the weather moderated.

The following day Mr. Cusack managed to prevail on some Malahide boatmen to cross to the island. With some difficulty the men succeeded in recovering the bodies of two young men and a boy. They reported that because of the high seas they had been unable to land on Lambay. The three bodies were placed in open coffins in case there were relatives who could identify them.

For some days there had been conflicting reports on the condition of the wreck. One optimistic dispatch proclaimed, "The vessel still holds together and, as there is a large quantity of timber on board, she may continue to do so." At the beginning of the week most accounts suggested that the ship could be raised. One Liverpool shipowner gave his opinion that, "If the *Tayleur* had been made of wood by this time we would have her hull selling for lucifer matches, instead of which the underwriters intend raising her." However, by Wednesday the Dublin newspapers were reporting that the gales had, "Carried away all the masts, rigging and spars leaving nothing to be seen except floating fragments. The coastguards continue to secure all that could be observed and got at." The question of salvage appeared to be out of the question. "We may add that the vessel is a total wreck and has gone to pieces. There appears little chance of the cargo of the vessel being saved."

In the next twenty-four hours the weather eased sufficiently to allow contact to be made with the coastguards on Lambay and determined efforts were made to reach the dead. The coroner at Malahide gave orders that the fifty-four then recovered were to be buried in the island's little graveyard. During the day forty-two coffins from a Dublin undertaker were delivered to the island. Eventually, about ninety bodies were found and all were interred on Lambay.

On Tuesday afternoon two hundred and twenty-three of *Tayleur*'s passengers, many dressed in ill-fitting clothes which had been collected by charitable groups in Dublin, left the Waterford Steamship Company's warehouse and proceeded to the North Wall to embark on the Prince for Liverpool. On the quay a large, silent crowd had assembled and as the steamer passed down river, there was a spontaneous, heart-felt cheer of encouragement. The survivors lined the *Prince's* rails and responded with shouts of gratitude and farewell. Half a dozen survivors had reached Liverpool a few hours earlier in the *Roscommon*.

At Liverpool the newspaper reporters were waiting and for the next few days the national press gave full coverage to the catastrophe and the local press continued to discuss the loss of the ship for weeks after the event. Much of the early reporting was inaccurate and it was not until the inquest and the official enquiries some time later that the true facts emerged.

The awful news of the loss of the *Tayleur* struck Warrington like a thunderclap. At first there was disbelief at reports that the strongest ship ever built had sunk. The *Warrington Guardian* editorial which was published nearly a week after the wreck conveys something of the doubt and uncertainty in the town when the first dispatch was received. "On Monday last a passenger on his way from Holyhead via Chester conveyed to the people of Warrington the astounding intelligence that the noble vessel *Tayleur* which, only a few months ago they had crowded to see launched, was a total wreck and somewhere about 400 of her passengers are no more. The news was not credited at first. To remove all doubts we dispatched a reporter to Liverpool and soon had a telegraphic message from him confirming the worst of tidings. We believe that she had about six hundred passengers. Five stowaways were also found after the tug left the ship."

The people of Warrington desperately wanted to hear reassuring information and the local press printed optimistic and unfounded reports that the ship could probably be salvaged. "Up to the present hour, though loose at the stern and buffeted by every wave, she holds fast together and yet may be raised." A great deal was written in praise of *Tayleur's* beauty, strength and swiftness. Her builders were lauded for their skill in constructing a ship which could withstand such damage and yet survive. "What does it speak for the wisdom of the heads which planned her and the strength of the brawny arms which rivetted her together. An American sailor who is amongst the saved says that if she had been made of wood she would assuredly have gone to pieces." But *Tayleur* had gone to pieces a couple of days before the newspaper article was written. The remains of the ship lay in deep water off the Nose promontory. An utter wreck, the vessel was inaccessible debris on the seabed.

The newspapers also reported that, "One or two parties from Warrington went out with the ill-fated vessel but their names or the fate which has befallen them is not known."

When the notice of a fund to aid *Tayleur's* destitute passengers was announced there was an immediate response. In addition to the money given to survivors by Lloyd's agent in Dublin, Pilkington and Wilson made each person an interim payment of ten shillings. The company also offered a free passage to Australia in another vessel or the return of the fare that had been paid for the passage in *Tayleur*. The survivors spoke highly of the generous treatment they had received from Pilkington and Wilson and there was much satisfaction when it was known that the firm had awarded Captain Dearl of the *Prince* the sum of twenty pounds for his kind attention to the passengers.

In Liverpool a subscription list was started and donors were asked to sign either at the Exchange Rooms or at the offices of Pilkington and Wilson. The ship's owners, Charles Moore and Company headed the subscriptions with a donation of £500 and generous donations of £100 were given by the shipping companies, James Baines and Company, Bright and Co. and Brown, Shipley and Company. Half a dozen firms gave £100 as did Pilkington and Wilson. The members of the Dublin Chamber of Commerce were unselfish in subscribing a sum which amounted to about £5 for each member. The Lord Mayor of Dublin contributed £10 to the appeal. Her Majesty's Colonial Land and Emigration Commissioners gave £50 to the appeal fund.

The *Tayleur's* builders, the Bank Quay Foundry donated £100 and the eventual purchasers of the wreck, Samuel Dutton and Nephew of Liverpool, contributed three guineas. The clerks in Pilkington and Wilson's office subscribed two guineas.

Within a week of the disaster the *Tayleur* Appeal had raised over £1,500 from seventy-eight subscribers. With Captain Schomberg R.N. as chairman and the Honourable Joseph Cunard, treasurer, the Committee for the Relief of *Tayleur* Sufferers resolved to approach the banks requesting them to allow subscription books to be opened in their branches. All claimants on the fund were asked to submit their claims for losses to the Committee at Her Majesty's Emigration Commissioner's Office in Bath Street. The renowned James Baines of the Black Ball line acted as secretary to the relief committee for the dependents of those who had perished in the wreck.

Some prominent firms and personalities were slow in coming forward with their donations and the *Liverpool Mercury* of 31st January noted that, "At the foot of the column of subscriptions appears the following, 'The members of the

Borough, the Mayor and several influential shipowners have yet to be seen.'"
In Dublin a distress fund was established for the survivors under the chairmanship of Lord Talbot de Malahide. The Distress Fund Committee announced that, "If more money be raised than may be required to meet the present emergency, the balance should remain as a Fund available at once for such Shipwrecked Strangers as may become future claimants on the generosity of the citizens of Dublin." After each of *Tayleur's* passengers had been paid an equitable sum there was money left over and this was used to relieve survivors of other shipwrecks on the Irish coast. The *Tayleur* Fund for the Succour of Shipwrecked Strangers also struck medals to be presented to those who had shown distinguished gallantry in saving life at sea.

IN MEMORY OF
THOMAS STOTT (aged 29),
AND
SARAH, HIS WIFE (aged 26),
Who Died January 21, 1854,
Having perished by the wreck of the Tayleur, off Lambay Island, on the Irish Coast, bound for Melbourne.
Elate with hope, with prospects bright,
They left their native shore;
Death stayed their progress o'er the wave—
They sank to rise no more,

The memorial card to a young couple who were drowned in the wreck of the 'Tayleur'.

Chapter Nine: The Enquiries

Within days of the wreck of the *Tayleur* and long before the facts had been established, the newspapers were publishing letters from armchair critics who had all the answers to the problems which Captain Noble had encountered. Some letters were absurd whilst many of those which referred to the foreign members of the crew were at least insensitive and occasionally, blatantly racist and abusive.

Racial discrimination is not a twentieth century phenomena. In the last century it was even more pronounced than it is today. It was an age when there was much bellicosity with John Bull roistering when foreign nationals were held to be of little account. The reports of the alleged wayward conduct of *Tayleur's* foreign crew members were grossly exaggerated and these stories have become myths which are still banded about to this day. The Victorian press remarked that, "Chinese and Lascar crew make very inefficient seamen in cold latitudes, the cold being so intense as to benumb them and make them incapable of performing any duty." Only three of the *Tayleur's* seamen were Chinese and the two 'lascars' in the crew were probably the cook and the passengers' steward, who both came from Bombay! Yet in an authoritative maritime history written a few years after the tragedy it was claimed that, "The crew was largely composed of Chinese and Lascar seamen who were far from satisfactory."

In another book of shipwrecks of the last century, the author was moved to make the following invidious comment on the three Chinese who managed to reach safety, "The Chinese and the Lascars caught the panic, these Orientals leaping for life in maniacal haste regardless of the shouted orders of the officers. Several of these paltroons contrived to scramble to safety and satisfied themselves with their own miserable lives without giving a thought to those left behind." In contrast, the European seamen who had managed to reach the rocks were, according to the author, unselfish and courageous. "They gave an illustration of national courage at its best, a striking proof of the temperamental differences between the Easterner and the Westerner – cowardice on one hand and self-sacrifice on the other. The action of *Tayleur's* crew has tinctured the seamen's outlook on the Oriental races to this present day – although they are admitted as sterling workers their courage is everlastingly questioned."

Something of the contempt felt for the Chinese survivors of the *Tayleur* can be ascertained from the crew list of those saved which was published a few days after the wreck. The men are not even afforded the dignity of a name. They appear in the newspaper reports as, "Abo, Abo and Abo, three Chinese seamen."

A correspondent signing himself "Sheridan" advocated the establishment of a free training school for foreign seamen where a captain could satisfy himself of the men's capabilities before engaging them. The writer thought that it was, "Very disheartening to those who had left their nation and embarked on a ship with all they possessed in the world, a countenance beaming with hope of reaching a country where success crowns the enterprising emigrant and within a short distance of the port of embarkation they find that the ship is not properly equipped and manned and their bright hopes for the future are dashed aside." The writer believed that if his suggestions were to be adopted, "I am sure that there would not be so many launched into eternity."

Both Captain Noble and his first mate were highly qualified seamen yet the very possession of qualifications prompted correspondents to write to the newspapers questioning the value of certificates and examinations. One irrational letter-writer who signed himself "Observer", believed that examinations were no guarantee for the safe navigation of a ship. "The ability to pass examinations and to obtain such a certificate might exert a deleterious influence and beget a self-satisfaction which stops improvement, stifles exertion and distorts judgement by the thought that so perfect a man need not trouble himself to learn more. To go through an examination successfully and obtain a certificate of ability has an inflating influence."

Some letters were malevolent in their condemnation of Captain Noble. "If any individual is to blame for the terrible disaster it is Captain Noble. Noble is an approved and certificated man. His first mate is certificated too. It is clear that the examination of Captain Noble and the certificates granted to Captain Noble and his mate failed to supply in the hour of need the caution, vigilance, discretion and prompt decision which could have easily prevented the disaster."

A correspondent writing to *"The Times"* called for the introduction of new machines for the testing of chain cables. The writer claimed that the existing apparatus for proving cables were merely tension machines which simply exerted a steady pull. New devices were needed which could simulate the force of a storm by snatching the chains in order to detect a weak link.

The debate on iron versus wood in ship construction was fully aired. Some correspondents blamed the *Tayleur's* builders. "She could not have been strong compared with her bulk, nor could she have been framed with proper water-tight compartments. If sufficiently constructed the blow on the rocks ought only to have damaged her locally."

Then there was a remedy for coping with a deficiency in crew numbers. "It is, or should be generally known that there is a mechanical contrivance whereby topsails are reefed or unreefed from the deck in a few minutes without the necessity of sending men aloft. The invention is due to a Mr. Cunningham of Gosport who declares that where his plan has been adopted three hands have been sufficient to reef the maintopsail of a 500-ton ship in two minutes and that the reefs can be shaken out from the deck with the same facility. It is tolerably clear that had the *Tayleur* been able to reduce her sails she would not have gone ashore."

The *Tayleur's* deck cabin or "camboose" as it was called at the time of her launch, was smashed by the seas. This prompted letters to the press. Typical is the following, "It is strange that a ship could be sent to sea with one of those fair weather cabins on deck – hurricane cabins we believe they are called – which may answer admirably for a run up and down the great rivers of the American continent but are totally unfitted for ocean navigation. Here were 150 persons washed overboard by a single sea in their frail receptacle just like poultry in a coup." Such inaccurate and exaggerated accounts of the sinking abound. These lurid yarns persisted even after the official report into the sinking had been published. One correspondent claimed that the *Tayleur* was an iron ship with the floating qualities of a cannon-ball and it was a matter of no surprise that she sank instantly when striking the rocks. Another writer said that as soon as the ship had been holed, "She assumed the buoyancy of a locomotive engine."

There were letters pointing out that it would be safer for sailing ships to be towed by steam tugs into the Atlantic and well clear of the narrow seas of the United Kingdom.

As to the recruiting of a ships' crews, one letter to *The Times* declared that no emigrant ship should leave port, "Until at least twenty-four hours after all the seamen have been on board with all their senses and faculties as clear as they are likely to be, and with the knowledge that every rope is in its proper place and how the ropes lead." The writer stated that the crew should be able to work the gear in daylight and at night. He said that such was the poor state of most ships' crews leaving Liverpool and other ports, "That it is a matter of surprise not how they go on the rocks but how they got clear of them."

There were many unfeeling savants who were wise after the event and who dashed off inane letters to the press but none of them were as unwholesome as the advertisement of a Mr. Hellewell, chandler of 53 Castle Street, Liverpool. Within a week of the first news of the loss of the *Tayleur* being received, Hellewell seized the opportunity to profit from the tragedy. His advertisement in the *Liverpool Mercury* proclaimed in large capital letters:-

> "LIFEBELTS, LIFEBELTS, LIFEBELTS
> LOSS OF *TAYLEUR* IN DUBLIN BAY
> UPWARDS OF 400 HUMAN BEINGS DROWNED.
> The whole of these unfortunate persons would have saved their lives had they been provided with one of
> **HELLEWELL'S LIFE AND PROPERTY BELTS,**
> ranging in price from seven shillings and sixpence each.
> Most invaluable at sea in case of shipwreck. Can be had wholesale and retail at his airproof and waterproof establishments."

The directors of the Maritime Assurance Company of Liverpool gave a generous donation of £50 to the committee which had been set up to relieve the suffering of *Tayleur*'s passengers and crew. At the same time the directors seized the opportunity of doing business. In a letter which was published in the press they stated that they had paid the donation, "To those, who unfortunately for themselves or their survivors, had neglected to avail themselves of the advantages offered by payment of a small premium to insure their lives against accident at sea." The directors pointed out that, "If mariners and passengers more generally take the precaution of insuring themselves against accident at sea the appeals to private benevolence, which are now so frequently made, would be unnecessary."

Back on Lambay the incessant stormy weather made it impossible to convene the coroner's inquest on Lambay and the hearing was held on the mainland at the Malahide Hotel in Malahide. The enquiry was conducted by the County Coroner, Mr. Henry Davies and many prominent local personages were summoned to serve as jurors. These included Lord Talbot de Malahide, six magistrates and a clergyman. A great number of friends and relatives of the deceased passengers crowded into the room, some attended by solicitors. Mr. Charles Barry as counsel with Mr. Thomas Fitzgerald, solicitor appeared for Mr. Carmichael of Glasgow who had lost his father, mother, brother and sister and there were lawyers representing Dublin families who had lost relatives in the disaster. Captain Walker R.N. attended the inquest on behalf of the Board of Trade as did Lieutenant Prior, the Assistant Emigration Officer of Liverpool. Mr.

W. Fitzgibbon Q.C. was instructed on behalf of Captain Noble.

The bodies of two of the victims had been brought to the hotel. They were those of Edward Kewley who was *Tayleur's* second mate and that of a young boy identified as the son of Dr. Cunningham, the ship's medical officer.

Captain Noble was subjected to a lengthy cross-examination during which he created a favourable impression by his direct and unhesitating replies to the questions put to him. He had the support of all his crew and the majority of the passengers who said that he had done all that was possible to save them after the ship struck the rocks.

The captain detailed the problems he had experienced with steering the ship although he insisted that every block and every rope in the vessel was in good working order. In reply to Lord Talbot de Malahide's suggestion that the newness of the tackle might have interfered with the working of the ship, Captain Noble's answer was a blunt denial. He said that he was surprised but not alarmed when he sighted land. Notwithstanding his experience with the steering on the previous night, he was sure that he had plenty of time to clear the coast. He said that he had commanded large ships before being appointed to command the *Tayleur* but he had never experienced difficulties steering them.

The question of compass variation and the lethal course followed after dropping the pilot occupied much of the enquiry. Noble stated that although the weather was hazy he was certain that he was proceeding down the Channel and therefore he did not think that it was necessary to change tack. He said, "I do not think that I stood too long on one tack. With a free wind that tack ought to have brought me to the equator." On the morning of the wreck he had examined the three compasses and was surprised at the extent of variation between them. He had made his calculations on the supposition that the compass before the helmsman was correct. Captain Noble admitted that he did not adopt the only means to enable him to get out of difficulty, namely by using the lead. He said that he did not do so because he did not think it necessary. To Captain Walker's question, "Do you think that you were wrong in not trying for soundings?" Noble replied, "I think that I did wrong and this will be a warning for me for the future." Walker commented, "Sad that such a melancholy experience should be bought so dear."

Captain Walker considered that it was strange that the owners of an iron ship with iron masts should have omitted the precaution of making certain that the vessel had her full cargo on board before the compasses were adjusted. As it was, the compasses were 'swung' or calibrated two months prior to sailing and before the cargo was taken in.

Captain Noble had no complaints to make about his crew. He insisted, "They were a good crew. I had them on board for three or four days before we sailed. I found my crew to work very well." As to undermanning, Noble said that he had enough seamen. To a juror who asked, "Would it have made a difference if you had ten more men on board?" He replied, "If I had a hundred additional men on board I could not have done any better."

The captain emphatically denied that he had asked any passengers to pull on the ropes saying that he had enough seamen on board to do all the necessary work.

Describing his desperate attempts to clear Lambay Captain Noble said that on sighting land he had made sail as quickly as possible by putting on extra canvas. He put on mizzenstaysail, maintopmast staysail and spanker but to no avail. "No matter what sail I had on I do not think the ship would have stayed as there was too much sea running. If I could have got her round on the other tack either by staying or wearing I would have got clear of the island. It was my only chance and all I could do was try it."

Captain Noble maintained that if the anchor cables had not parted the ship would have been saved, but because of the heavy seas running onto a lee shore from the whole breadth of the Channel it was expecting too much of them to hold.

Of the ship's final moments the captain said that everything possible had been done to save the lives of the passengers. He said that he would have cut down the wooden foremast to provide a bridge to the shore and by this means he thought it possible that as many as nine-tenths of the passengers could have been saved. Unfortunately, he was unable to carry out his plan because of the panic on deck. "From the manner in which the passengers were crowding about and the confusion I was not able to cut it away. It would have killed more than were drowned." He added that he did not order the boats to be lowered because, "It would have been injudicious to do so seeing the state of the sea." Captain Noble said that he had hung onto a rope after all the passengers had left the vessel and that he only left the ship when she was under water.

In reply to Mr. Holland's assertion that he had helped the crew because he saw that they were shorthanded, Captain Noble said that although he remembered seeing Holland on board he did not see him assisting the crew. No passenger had assisted the crew and it was untrue that he had made derogatory remarks about his men. Noble said that he had received no reports of crew members sleeping in the cradle.

The captain stated that he believed *Tayleur's* rudder was probably too small for such a large ship and that this contributed to the loss of the vessel but he maintained that the primary reason of the disaster was the malfunctioning of the compasses. He did not think that the position of the boats on the davits had an influence on the ship's performance. He told the enquiry that he did not go to bed or take off his clothes from the time the vessel left Liverpool.

Michael Murphy, the first mate, said that the ship's log had been lost in the wreck but that he had read one that Captain Noble had prepared from memory and he believed it to be accurate. Murphy was an experienced officer with a master's certificate. He estimated that there were twenty good able seamen out of the twenty-three on board the ship. He found some of the foreigners – not the able seamen – skulking and he reported them to the captain. Murphy said that he, "Found the crew to be a very fair crew. Part of them were very good men." The mate declared that he heard no complaints from passengers relating to the efficiency of the crew. He did not think the vessel was undermanned. The mate said that he had observed slight differences in the compasses on Friday and that the variations had increased considerably by eight o'clock on Saturday morning.

The third mate, Hugh Cowan, had acted with bravery in assisting the passengers during the ship's final moments but he was very ill at ease in the coroner's court. He became confused when pressed about events that had occurred early in the voyage. He was uncertain about times, distances and the identification of coastal lights. On one detail however, he was definite and that was the variation between the compasses. Of the crew Cowan said that whilst the men were under his charge he found them to be, "Good and efficient."

Lieutenant Prior of the Emigration Commission said that it was his duty to see that emigration ships were properly fitted out and that they were fully manned. He said that he went aboard the *Tayleur* on the day before she sailed and he declared that he had never seen a ship so well fitted out. Prior said that the crew was, "Perfectly competent to work the vessel." He had arrived at this conclusion after the briefest of contacts with the men – no more than a couple of hours at most. He admitted, "The only opportunity I had of knowing whether the crew could reef and steer was by their answering my questions." He stressed that he had had nothing to do with procuring the crew.

The complete absence of State supervision during the construction of merchant vessels in the mid-nineteenth century meant that ships were not subjected to strict tests of seaworthiness. They put to sea for the first voyage without any inspection to see if the plating was sound and it was to be another twenty years before the introduction of the Plimsoll maximum load-line. The size of deck cargoes was not limited.

Lieutenant Prior told the enquiry that the *Tayleur* had been "surveyed" two months before she sailed and he did not think it was necessary for her to have undergone sea trials because, "A ship built on scientific principles ought to have her rudder right. I would have no objection to taking a new ship to sea without a trial." The Lieutenant made no comment on the size of the ship's rudder or on its patent semi-automatic steering mechanism.

Questioned about the ship's compasses, Prior said that Mr. Gray who had adjusted them was a first-rate man in his business and if Captain Noble had doubts about the accuracy of the compasses during the voyage he should have used the lead. Prior declared, "I would have sounded myself. I always did."

It is a matter of some surprise that no mention was made of the possible effect the small steam-boat which was secured to *Tayleur's* deck, could have had on the compasses. Although this was a wooden-hulled craft it was complete with its engine and it was built with iron fastening bolts.

The steamer's funnel had been removed to be stowed away inside the boat. The vessel was lashed from the break of the poop to the mainmast on the starboard side and was positioned about eight feet from the forward compass and thirty-three feet from the binnacle compass.

A Captain Kerr R.N. was called. When asked his views on the importance of using the lead he said that it was the captain's duty to take soundings from the moment the pilot left. Kerr said that if Captain Noble had used the twenty fathom line at six o'clock on the Saturday morning he would have found, by consulting the chart, exactly where he was.

Captain Kerr was emphatic on the question of the compasses. He said that if he (Captain Kerr) had suspected that his compasses were wrong and at the same time his ship would not answer the helm he would have returned to port as the responsibility to go on was too great.

Kerr told the enquiry that there was something seriously wrong with a ship which took an hour to tack and which drifted five miles to leeward whilst doing so but he did not think that the newly-made gear had been an obstacle in the working of the ship. In his opinion Captain Noble, "Did all that skill and seamanship could suggest to save the lives of the passengers under the circumstances."

Mr. George Finlay, the Lambay coastguard gave evidence which fully supported Captain Noble's assertion that on the morning of the wreck the visibility was very poor. Finlay said that the weather was so obscure that he could not see the top of the island from his cottage nor could he see the water from the top of the island. He doubted that a lifeboat could have survived in the heavy seas running at the time. In his statement the coastguard said that it was untrue that he had said that, "It was a lubberly thing for a captain to bring a ship to where she struck." He had merely remarked that it was strange to see a ship in such a place.

Practically every witness paid tribute to the courage displayed by Captain Noble. It was said that the conduct of Captain Noble during the whole period of the awful emergency was "praiseworthy in the extreme". However, the captain had his critics. Foremost among these was Robert Holland, the wealthy passenger, who owned two yachts and who undoubtedly knew something about ship handling. Holland gave examples of what he considered to be crew inefficiency and he insisted that the vessel was not handled properly and that the ship was undermanned.

Mr. Davies, the coroner, recorded the following verdict; "That the parties were drowned by the sinking of the said ship off Lambay Island, and that this deplorable accident occurred in consequence of the highly culpable neglect of the owners in permitting the vessel to leave port without the compasses being properly adjusted or a sufficient trial having taken place to learn whether she was under the control of the helm or not. We find that Captain Noble did not take sufficient precaution to ensure the safety of the vessel by sounding after he found the compasses were in error but we consider that from the time the vessel came in sight of land that he acted with coolness and courage and used every exertion in his power to save the lives of the passengers."

The Coroner also expressed the opinion that the authorities should insist that the shipping companies' should have the same manning levels in their vessels as was the practice on ships which were chartered by the government for the purposes of emigration and the conveyance of government stores. The newspaper account of the inquest ends with the following comment, "Captain Noble was not criminally impugned by the verdict."

Within ten days of the loss of the *Tayleur* Mr. J.P. Palmer, the chairman of the Liverpool Underwriter's Association, one of the principal insurers of the ship, issued a statement. Palmer said that after enquiries at the Sailors' Home from where the crew had been shipped, his company expressed satisfaction with the crew and expressed no complaint against the owners of the vessel even though the underwriters would have been relieved of all responsibility if the *Tayleur* could have been shown to have been poorly manned or undermanned.

John Grantham, a prominent naval architect and inspector of iron ships visited the wreck on behalf of the underwriters and the Board of Trade. He was accompanied by a Mr. Rennie who was, almost certainly, Mr. William Rennie who designed the *Tayleur*. Grantham's report to the underwriters dismissed the possibility that design faults had contributed to the loss of the vessel. Interestingly though, Grantham was consultant engineer to the Bank Quay Foundry where he supervised the construction of the *Sarah Palmer* which was launched in 1855. Could he also have had a role in overseeing the building of *Tayleur*?

On 7th February a *Liverpool Mercury* article reported on the condition of the ship. The divers reported that the vessel had struck pointed rocks as she lay broadside against the cliff. The rocks were described as, "Quite sufficient to tear open any vessel of wood or iron." The ship was found to be parted at the stern and the decks had been forced upwards, the cargo being strewn on the sea bed.

On the same day it was reported in *Lloyd's List* that wreckage from the *Tayleur* consisting mostly of deals, battens and prepared boards had been washed on the Cumbrian coast near Maryport and a few days later beds, bedding, clothes, empty casks and barrels drifted ashore at Girvan on the Firth of Clyde. In the days that followed, the tides of the Irish Sea even carried some small fragments of the cargo back to the Mersey estuary.

Shipwreck with appalling loss of life was a frequent occurrence in the days of the sailing ship but the loss of the *Tayleur* on her maiden voyage had a profound impact on Victorian society. The newspapers proclaimed the disaster to be as great a catastrophe as the loss of the iron troopship *Birkenhead* two years previously and the public avidly awaited the official report into the wreck.

Captain Walker of the Board of Trade submitted his report to both Houses of Parliament. He said that the *Tayleur* was a beautiful vessel, well-built and massively framed having five distinct watertight compartments each of which had a separate well and sounding pipe. The ship was class A1 at Lloyds and she was abundantly equipped with stores.

Of the ship's complement, Captain Walker stated that the number of crew was insufficient but he said that this objection would apply to a very large number of emigrant ships which managed to reach their destinations without mishap.

Although the tonnage laws for ships had been changed in 1836, many builders continued to give the 'old' measurements for their vessels twenty or thirty years after the new registry act had been introduced. This could have a significant effect on manning levels. Captain Walker pointed out that in the case of the *Tayleur* the usage of the Port of Liverpool had been complied with. This required three crew members for every hundred tons. He confirmed that by the old system of measurement the ship displaced 1,640 tons but by the new system of measurement the ship was 1,979 tons. Lieutenant Prior had calculated manning levels according to the old rules which, declared Walker, were absurd and which ought to be abolished.

Captain Walker stressed the fact that the Emigration Commissioners demanded four crew for every hundred tons on all their vessels and he said that this should be the manning level on emigrant ships. He reasoned that when one considers the length of a voyage, the journey through the tropics, heavy weather and the possibility of members of the crew being on the sick list then three men for every hundred tons was insufficient.

However, Walker insisted that the loss of the *Tayleur* was not due to undermanning. He stated explicitly, "I do not think that the crew were in any way implicated in the loss of the vessel." However, he felt that he had to report the fact that, "Two witnesses hazarded a contrary opinion."

Captain Walker reported that the loss of the ship was due solely to the fact that the compasses were not in proper order. He maintained that this catastrophe had occurred through the ship's master making his calculations on the supposition that the compass before the helmsman was correct. He observed that it was strange that Captain Noble did not use the obvious means to find his way out of difficulty – by using the lead.

At another enquiry, judgement was passed on *Tayleur's* master, the experienced and accomplished certificated master-mariner who had lost the finest merchant ship afloat within forty-eight hours of the vessel leaving port on her first voyage. At a special meeting held before the local Marine Board of Liverpool in the Sailors' Home in Canning Place, the future of Captain Noble was decided. The enquiry lasted nearly a month and many witnesses were called. The captain was subjected to an interrogation to determine whether he was competent to perform the duties of a ship's master under the terms of the Merchant Marine Act.

The Marine Board's findings were presented to the Board of Trade and of Captain Noble the following conclusion was reached, "The Board is fully impressed with the conviction that Captain Noble, notwithstanding the serious disaster with which his name is connected, possesses skill and ability both as a navigator and as a seaman and they have therefore, no hesitation in reporting to my Lords their unanimous opinion that John Noble is neither from incompetency nor from any other cause, unfit to discharge the duties of a master and therefore recommend to my lords the renewal of his certificate of competency."

The Liverpool Board found that the *Tayleur* had been lost through the deviation of her compasses, the cause of which they were unable to determine. The Board called attention to the many cases of compasses being in error on both wood and iron ships which were navigating in the Irish Sea. It was pointed out that these frequent phenomena, "Are not accounted for by any theory at present. They therefore strongly recommend all ship's masters to doubt the accuracy of their compasses and to adopt every means in their power to check and test them."

The fact that compasses in iron ships could show false readings was not news on Merseyside. Indeed the problem was causing much anxiety at John Lairds, the builders of iron ships at Birkenhead. For some years the company had been conducting an investigation to determine the cause of compass failure. Lairds had even gone to the trouble of obtaining the services of the Astronomer Royal, Professor Airey, and had placed at his disposal their 600 ton iron paddle steamer *'Rainbow'* . However Airey's experiments did not supply a solution and the menace of compass deception remained unsolved for another twenty years.

Although the Malahide inquest and the Liverpool enquiry into the loss of the *Tayleur* gave the reason for the disaster as being solely due to compass error, the newspapers continued to make much of the alleged inefficiency of the crew. Some of the press statements at the time were patently ridiculous but they are still being repeated in modern maritime histories. A recent study holds that, "The crew was largely composed of Chinese and Lascar seamen who were far from satisfactory." It is an absurdity to state that three Chinese ordinary seamen and two Indians or 'lascars' who were passengers' servants could have played any significant part in working the ship. More likely to be true is the popular folk legend which claimed that sea sprites lured the ship onto the rocks in order to favour the Ships' Carpenters' Association whose members lamented the use of iron instead of oak in ship construction.

But was the *Tayleur's* crew as competent as Captain Noble had claimed or were his favourable comments intended to procure the men's tacit support at the inquest and at the enquiries? The contemporary accounts of the abilities of the seamen are so varied that it is difficult to reach a decision. Certainly, the crew were a desultory group of individuals some of whom were too young to have had much sea-going experience. Very few of them lost their lives in the wreck. Only six crew members out of the complement of seventy-one were drowned. Did they make good their escape as soon as they could without a thought for the passengers? The question of crew discipline, composure and proficiency remains a matter in dispute to this day.

There were other aspects of the catastrophe that were never fully explored. No investigation seems to have taken place to ascertain the performance of the ship's patent rudder mechanism. Was her rudder too small? It was said that the ship was to have been a steamer but as the engine builders were too busy with full order books, the vessel was hurriedly rigged as a sailing vessel. Did the modifications which took place after the ship's plans went from the designer to the builder have any effect on the *Tayleur's* sailing efficiency?

The loss of the *Tayleur* did not have an adverse effect upon the career of her designer, William Rennie. Indeed, two years after the wreck an article appeared in the Liverpool newspaper *'Albion'*, describing Rennie's work on another ship, stating that, 'Mr Rennie is celebrated as the finest marine draughtsman in England'. After moving to London, Rennie went on to design many more vessels including half a dozen tea clippers as well as a number of screw and paddle steamers. Shipbuilders from every part of Britain consulted Rennie. By 1856 he was consulting engineer to the Royal Mail Packet Company and he was a partner in the firm of Rennie and Marshall, shipbuilders and repairers of King and Queen Dock at Rotherhithe. William Rennie was still engaged in ship design and shipbuilding into his late sixties. He enjoyed enormous prestige throughout a long career

The enquiries could offer no explanation as to why the compasses had failed. Did the loading of cargo after the compasses were adjusted cause them to deviate or did the variation occur because of the proximity of the river steamer chained to the deck?

A Mr. William Thompson, later to be the famous scientist Lord Kelvin, wrote to *The Times* giving his opinion that the *Tayleur* had been built on the stocks with her head to the north and the riveters had hammered what might be called "northern magnetism" into the hull and the compasses were adjusted to allow for that. When the ship sailed southwards down the Irish Channel the original "northern magnetism" was knocked out of her by the storm waves and this resulted in the compasses giving false readings.

One outcome of *Tayleur's* fate was the formation of the Liverpool Compass Committee. The Committee had the quays marked with compass readings which allowed ships' masters to check their compasses before leaving port. The marks could still be used today.

The adjustment of the compasses in iron ships was little understood and between 1855 and 1860 the Liverpool Compass Committee submitted three reports to the Board of Trade. Nathaniel Hawthorne was also concerned at the mysterious compass deviation which he thought occurred only in American ships which were operating in the Irish Sea. He informed Washington of his anxieties. In one dispatch he concluded that there had to be some connection between the manner of stowing cargo and the resulting compass deviation.

The enquiries were kind to Captain Noble. His Master's Certificate was renewed allowing him to resume his career. He was in command of the *Earl of Sefton* which was destroyed by fire in 1859. Once again, Noble was cleared of negligence and his Master's certificate was renewed but strange to say, the Board of Trade did not renew his Extra-Master's certificate until 21st January 1860 – six years to the day after the sinking of the *Tayleur* !

There is so much one would like to know about some of those who survived the wreck. What was the subsequent history of Samuel Carley and his wife and son? Did they eventually settle in Australia? It would be interesting to learn what happened to the frightened passenger who jumped onto the tug and was brought back to Liverpool. Then there was the woman who was put ashore with her daughter because they were deemed unfit. What future did they have? And the "ocean child" who was rescued after his parents drowned? The riddle was solved when the baby was identified allowing the Reverend Mr. Armstrong to locate the child's relatives into whose care he surrendered the infant. Did he have a happy childhood? Did he prosper in life?

There was a satisfactory outcome for at least one survivor, for the gallantry of miner George Lewis, who had assisted in the rescue of about fifteen fellow passengers was recognised. Lewis had lost everything in the wreck. The committee of the Liverpool Shipwreck and Humane Society awarded him £10. It was reported that Lewis "returned to Methyr Tydfil on Friday, his wife having been subject to violent fits ever since hearing of the loss of *Tayleur*".

The majority of *Tayleur's* passengers were young folk. Some couples had married only weeks before setting out for Australia. John Clough, the son of the landlord of the "Boar's Head" inn in Hyde, Manchester and his wife were married just five days before the ship sailed. They were both drowned. There were no further references in the newspapers to "the parties" from Warrington who had sailed in the ill-fated ship. No doubt they saw the vessel building on the stocks and perhaps they had witnessed the joyous moment of her launch. They were also to see the agony of the ship's destruction. Did they survive? We do not know.

We do not know how many of those who survived the wreck of the *'Tayleur'* eventually settled and raised families in Australia but without doubt the story of the great iron clipper *'Tayleur'* forms part of the family history of many present-day Australians.

Postscript

In June the wreck of the *Tayleur* was offered for sale by auction at the offices of Messrs. Cunard, Mann and Company, shipbrokers of Liverpool. By the conditions of sale, the owners of the vessel did not guarantee to the purchasers the right to any goods, treasure or effects that were aboard the ship. As for the cargo, Mr. T. Shannon of Dublin entered into an agreement whereby he would attempt to salvage the goods receiving fifty per cent of the value of any property recovered. By the day of the auction Shannon had already landed bales of cloth which were announced for public sale in Dublin.

Shannon said that he was ready to recommence the salvage operation when the weather improved. His presence at the site of the wreck was not welcomed by those intending to bid for the ship. They complained that he had the advantage of being first on the scene and he could hinder attempts by the purchaser of the ship to recover the vessel's fittings. This argument influenced the bidding and the wreck of the *Tayleur* was knocked down to Messrs. Dutton and Nephew of Liverpool for the sum of £480. The purchase included the ship's cordage, canvas, chains and cable as well as the ship itself. Thus, the finest merchant ship built in England was sold within nine months of her launch for one seventieth of her building costs.

In the spring when the weather had moderated it was reported that two steam tugs and a sloop had appeared at the site of the wreck to begin the attempt to salvage the ship's cargo.

The subsequent story of Warrington's shipbuilding industry is brief. Charles Tayleur did not long survive his wife for he died within six months of the loss of the great ship named in his honour. Before the end of the year, Mr Heathcote, the foundry's resouceful manager, also died.

A number of ocean-going vessels of lesser size than *Tayleur* were to be launched from the Bank Quay yard but, two years after the wreck of the great clipper, shipbuilding ended in Warrington. By 1855 the shipping companies were demanding vessels of greater dimensions and such ships could not be launched into the upper Mersey.

For many years now there has been no commercial traffic on the upper reaches of the river Mersey. The lighthouse at Halehead, which was built early in this century, remains, but its light is long extinguished.

Today nothing is left of the Bank Quay Foundry and it is difficult to find the site of the works. The only evidence of shipbuilding in Warrington is to be found in the town's museum. Here, there is a box containing several pieces of ribbon – the christening tapes of vessels launched at Bank Quay a hundred and fifty years ago. One short length of faded pink ribbon is all that is left from the joyous occasion when, to the cheers of thousands, the *Tayleur* left the slipway at the start of her first and last voyage.

Not long after the tragedy, changes occurred in the management of the White Star Line. In 1856 John Pilkington retired from the partnership and Henry Wilson and his new partner, John Cunningham, ran the company until 1867 when financial difficulties forced them to sell the flag and goodwill to Thomas Henry Ismay. Under Ismay's leadership the White Star Line grew in size and importance to become one of the world's great shipping companies.

It is an undisputed fact that history repeats itself but the coincidences which occurred in the most legendary maritime disaster of all time are truly remarkable. In 1912 the Cunard White Star liner *Titanic* sank with the loss of 1,523 lives. Like the *Tayleur* the *Titanic* was a brand-new vessel on her maiden voyage. Both ships were operated by the White Star Line. The *Tayleur* was proclaimed the strongest and safest vessel of her day. *Titanic* was said to be unsinkable. Both vessels were divided into water-tight compartments. It was predicted that the ships would attain the highest speed to become the fastest vessels on their respective routes. On the stern of both ships the port of registry was Liverpool. When disaster struck, the passengers on both vessels were far from outside help.

For many months after her loss the Victorian newspapers continued to ponder the tragedy of the *Tayleur*. In the case of the *Titanic,* the ship still commands headlines in today's press. The loss of both vessels resulted in the adoption of additional safety features for all passenger ships leaving British ports.

The wrecks of both ships were discovered many years after their sinkings. For some years now the discovery of the *Titanic* and the recovery of objects from the ocean bed has excited public interest. For over a hundred years the wreck of the *Tayleur* remained undisturbed until 1957 when members of the Irish Sub-aqua club located the ship. The remains of the vessel are close to The Nose and a rock slide. She has slipped into deeper water and was discovered when divers found an anchor chain which led them directly to the ship.

The wreck of the *Tayleur* remains undivided and it consists of iron plates collapsed in on the frames. The masts are conspicuous being about a metre in diameter and with a ten metre length remaining. All around the vessel the sea bed is littered with fragments of willow pattern pottery from the cargo.

In the Maritime Museum in Dun Laoghaire in Ireland, there are some objects from the wreck. These include delft plates from a dinner service, a large jar which has the inscription "Bristol. Reg. 13 March 1842" and a manufacturer's metal nameplate from a donkey engine which was made by the Bank Quay Foundry Company in 1853. Some items of pottery, brass dog collars, cosmetics and bedroom toilet sets are deposited in the Civic Museum in Dublin together with the ship's bell, a binnacle, portholes, part of the steering mechanism and some improved cabin sanitary ware. Also in the Dublin Museum is the builder's half model of the ship's hull. One of the *Tayleur*'s anchors is on display in the main street of Rush.

Over the years divers have recovered many small items from the wreck and some pottery has found its way into Dublin's antique shops. On display in Liverpool's Maritime Museum is an attractive vegetable dish and a blue and white cup and saucer as well as a couple of corroded fittings from the ship.

Perhaps, at some time in the future, serious attempts will be made to discover what remains of the ship's cargo. She must still contain many interesting artifacts of mid-nineteenth century workmanship – evidence of the time when Britain was "The Workshop of the World".

The 'Tayleur' monument at Rush, seventeen miles from Dublin. Tayleur's anchor was presented to the town by Drogheda Sub-Aqua Club.

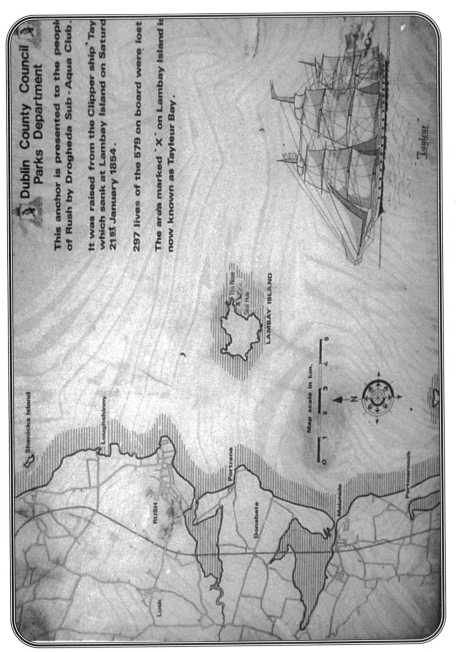

Dublin County Council
Parks Department

This anchor is presented to the peopl
of Rush by Drogheda Sub-Aqua Club.

It was raised from the Clipper ship 'Tay
which sank at Lambay Island on Saturd
21st January 1854.

297 lives of the 579 on board were lost

The area marked 'X' on Lambay Island i
now known as Tayleur Bay.

LAMBAY ISLAND

Map scale in km.

N

Shenicks island

Loughshinny

RUSH

Lusk

Portrane

Donabate

Malahide

Portmarnock

"Tayleur"

The plaque on the 'Tayleur' memorial at Rush.

An aerial view of Lambay Island showing, upper centre, Lord Talbot de Malahide's "castle" with the coastguard houses adjacent to the harbour. The feature in the circle to the right of the centre of the photograph is the tiny church and graveyard where many of the victims are buried.

THE TAYLEUR FUND MEDALS

Instituted in 1854 Tayleur Fund medals were awarded for eight separate rescues. The first medals were awarded in 1861 and the last for a rescue in 1875. In December 1913 the residue of the Tayleur Fund amounting to £1,500 was transferred to the RNLI and the issue of medals ceased.

Most of the Tayleur medals were struck in silver. There were two gold medals minted in addition to thirty-nine in silver. There is also a record of a copper and a bronze example, which were not awarded or inscribed.

The Tayleur medal is 45 millimetres in diameter and it has a dark blue ribbon. On the obverse side there is an impression of *Tayleur* breaking up on the rocks of Lambay. Around the circumference of the medal is the legend "Tayleur Fund For The Succour Of Shipwrecked Strangers" The reverse side is plain to be engraved with the recipient's name and the occasion of the award. The reverse side also bears the name of the chairman of the Fund Committee - Lord Talbot de Malahide.

Mr. John Walsh, Lloyd's Agent in Dublin, who had organised the rescue of *Tayleur's* survivors on Lambay in 1854 was himself to receive a gold Tayleur Fund medal seven years later. Mr.Walsh was involved in the rescue of crew members from a vessel which was being battered by a storm of hurricane force at Kingstown in 1861 He received severe lacerations-and had to be carried from the scene of the wreck. His friends placed him in a cab to take him to a doctor but the cab man refused to take him saying that Mr Walsh's blood would ruin the cab's upholstery. However, Mr.Walsh's gallantry had been witnessed by many and an irate crowd knocked the cab man to the ground and seized the cab to convey the injured man to the doctor. John Walsh was also awarded Lloyd's Silver Medal For Life Saving.

The Tayleur Fund Medal

IRON SHIPBUILDING IN WARRINGTON

The earliest record of iron shipbuilding at Warrington dates from 1840 when small iron paddle-steamers and a couple of schooners intended for use on the Mersey, were constructed at the Bridge Foundry.

The first iron vessels to be built at the Bank Quay shipyard were two schooners which were launched on the same tide in 1846. About 1850 the Bank Quay Foundry was extended and a short-lived programme of large ship construction was begun. For about four years ocean-going vessels were built in Warrington but by 1857 the venture was at an end. The advertisements for 'Premises to Let' for the Bank Quay Foundry appeared in the press in November 1857 and from then until the following January the machinery and the shipbuilding equipment were sold off.

The Bank Quay Foundry and shipyard were situated close to the London and North Western Railway station where there was a bend in the Mersey which allowed sufficient space for the launches to take place.

The company names for the Bank Quay yard were Tayleur, Sanderson and Company 1846; Tayleur and Company 1853; Bank Quay Foundry Company in 1856.

IRON VESSELS BUILT AT BANK QUAY FOUNDRY, WARRINGTON

Built	Vessel	Type	Tonnage	Owners
1846	*Enterprise*	Schooner	74	Used on the River Mersey
1846	*Neptune*	Schooner	70	Used on the River Mersey
1849	*Trout*	Schooner	58	
1852	*Invincible*	Paddle- Steamer	66	
1853	*La Perlita*	Screw- Steamer	84	Pacific Steam Navigation Co
1853	*Tayleur*	Ship	1979	C.Moore and Co.,Liverpool.
1854	*Lady Octavia*	Ship	1272	Adams & Co.,Greenock
1854	*Medora*	Barque	392	G.W.Turner, Liverpool
1854	*Deerslayer*	Barque	500	Blythe
1855	*Conference*	Ship	531	H.Moore,Liverpool
1854	*Liverpooliana**	Ship	800	C.Moore and Co.,Liverpool.
1855	*Retriever*	Barque	410	
1855	*Startled Fawn*	Ship	1165	G.H.Fletcher, Liverpool
1855	*Sarah Palmer*	Ship	1301	Palmer and Co.
1857	*Sarah Sands*	Ship		

* Name changed to *"Medora"* when sold to Shallcross and Company.
The *"Warrington Guardian"* of 29th April !854 gives a ship called *"Golden Vale"* which was nearing completion. This vessel does not appear in Lloyd's registers or the Liverpool Shipping Registers and it must be assumed that she was given another name.

WHITE STAR AUSTRALIAN PACKETS OF THE 1850s

Built	Ship	Tons	Builders
1849	*Iowa*	879	H.Irwin, St.John,New Brunswick
1851	*Bhurtpoor*	978	W.& R.Wright, St.John.
1847	*David Cannon*	1331	"
1852	*Fitzjames*	1195	Richibucto
1852	*Jessie Munn*	733	New Brunswick.
1853	*Arabian*	980	J.Nevins,St.John,New Brunswick
1853	*Red Jacket*	2305	C. Thomas, Rockland, Me.
1853	*Mermaid*	1321	McDonald,St.John,New Brunswick.
1853	*Emma*	1049	W.Bennett,Hopewell,New Brunswick
1853	*Golden Era*	1556	Smith & Haws,St.John.
1853	*Tayleur*	1979	Tayleur ,Warrington
1853	*Chariot of Fame*	2050	D.McKay,Boston, USA.
1854	*White Star*	2340	W.& R.Wright, St.John
1855	*Shepherdess*	1126	"
1854	*Annie Wilson*	1191	"
1853	*Prince of the Seas*	1316	J.Smith,St.John,New Brunswick
1858	*Blue Jacket*	986	McLachlan,Carleton,New Brunswick
1852	*Carntyne*	940	New Brunswick

APPENDICES
Bibliography

Annual Register 1854

Anderson, R. *White Star.* Stephenson. Prescot 1964

Bassett-Lowke W.J. and Holland G. *Ships and men.* G. Harrop. London 1946

Bach, John. *A Maritime History of Australia.* Hamish Hamilton. 1976

Bourke,E. *Shipwrecks of the Irish Coast.* Dublin North 1993

Corbett, J. *The River Irwell.* Abel Heywood and Son. Manchester 1906

Ferguson, S. *Growing up in Victorian Britain.* B.T. Batsford. London 1977

Hyde, F.E. *Liverpool and the Mersey.* David and Charles. Newton Abbot 1971

Kemp, Peter. *The History of Ships.* Orbis Publishing. London 1978

Lane, Tony. *Liverpool Gateway of Empire.* Lawrence and Wishart. London 1987

Lubbock, Basil. *The Colonial Clippers.* Brown Son and Ferguson. Glasgow 1968

MacGregor, David. *British and American Clippers.* Conway Press 1998

MacGregor, David. *Fast Sailing Ships 1775 – 1875.* Nautical Publishing Lymington 1988

May, Robin. *The Gold Rushes.* William Luscombe. London 1977

Mays, James. *Mr Hawthorne Goes to England.* Ringwood, Hampshire 1983

Rickard, John. *Australia. A Cultural History.* Longman. Harlow 1988

Roberts, David. *Cammell Laird - the golden years.* Avid Publications, Merseyside. 1998

Woodman, Richard. *The History of the Ship.* Conway Maritime Press. London 1997

Woods, E.A. *The White Star Sailing Packets.* Transactions of the Lancashire and Cheshire. Historical Society Vol. 96 (1944)

Newspapers and Journals

Dublin Evening Mail

Freemans Journal

Lancashire Life.

Liverpool Courier

Liverpool Mercury

Lloyds List

Sea Breezes. The Loss of the *Tayleur.* A.C. Wardle. New Series Vol. 2 1946

The Times

The Illustrated Liverpool News

The Illustrated London News

Warrington Guardian
Warrington Gazette

Other Sources

Port of Liverpool. The Customs Bills of Entry 1854
Transactions of the Old Dublin Society. Two Irish Sea Disasters. A.E.J. West. Dec. 1978

It is possible that an accurate list of those lost in the disaster has never been compiled. The contemporary newspaper accounts vary considerably both as to the number of people on board the ship and those lost in the disaster. At the Dublin inquest Mr Marcus McCausland, who had signed the ship's clearance certificate in Liverpool, stated that there were 488 passengers, 64 crew members and six apprentices aboard the vessel.

Three days after the wreck the *Liverpool Mercury* reported that a notice had been posted in the underwriters' room in Liverpool listing 488 passengers with an additional "sixteen first class passengers in cabin rooms".

Three weeks after the catastrophe the newspapers were in agreement that 290 had lost their lives. The Annual Register for 1854 concurs with this figure. However the monument at Rush records a death toll of 297 persons.

In the following appendices lists of people missing, unaccounted for and saved is a compilation made from the provisional lists which appeared in *The Times* and the *Liverpool Mercury* within a couple of days of the catastrophe. First names and ages are given if known.

The list of those lost is 360 names, sixty-three more than the number of deaths inscribed on the Rush memorial. Some of this large discrepancy might be explained by the fact that when the muster roll of the survivors was taken there were some passengers who were still in hospital in Dublin whilst other survivors did not return to Liverpool and therefore they were not registered amongst those saved.

Whatever the true facts, one thing is certain - the findings of every future enquiry into the loss of the *'Tayleur'* will produce a death toll that differs from those given in all previous investigations.

Passengers and crew unaccounted for and presumed lost.

Surname	Other Names	Age	Surname	Other Names	Age
AISLABIE	Mrs		CLOUGH	JOHN	28
AISLABIE	child		CLUTTICK	WILLIAM	30
ALLISON	JAMES	20	CLUTTICK	MRS	36
ANATOLE	V C	43	CLUTTICK	JANE	24
ANDERSON	WILLIAM M	24	CLUTTICK	CHARLES	36
ANDERSON	ALEXANDER	18	CLYVER	B.F	29
ANDREWS	JAMES	24	CODD	Mr	
ANDREWS	ELIZABETH	22	COLES	JOHN	21
ANDREWS	JOHN	INFANT	COLLINS	JOSEPH	20
ANDREWS	WILLIAM	28	COLTRAM ?	THOMAS	13
ANNING	HENRY	21	COMERS	THOMAS	24
ASHBURNER	CATHERINE	33	COOK	JOHN	34
ASHBURNER	MARY	INFANT	CORLEY	A	26
AUFORTH	JOHN	18	CRAWFORD	CHARLES	22
AUGUSTA	L	45	CROSTON	MARY	23
BAILIFF	MARGARET	30	CROSTON	EDWIN	INFANT
BALL	Family of 13		CUDDY	WILLIAM	42
BEATTY	JOHN	25	CUNNINGHAM	DR. HENRY H	
BETTA/BETTS	GEORGE	17	CUNNINGHAM	WIFE	
BLAIR	SAMUEL	30	CUNNINGHAM	CHILD	
BLAIR	JOHN	22	CUNNINGHAM		INFANT
BOAR	ALEXANDER	21	CURRAN	M	32
BOAR	MARY	28	CUTTS	MARTHA	30
BOAR	ROBERT	11	DAVIES	WALTER	42
BOAR	MARGARET	3	DAVISON	RICHARD	26
BOAR	JANET	8	DAWE/ DAWLE	D	25
BOAR	JANE	10	DAWSON	MRS	
BOAR	HUGH	19	DENTON	MARY A	26
BOAR	MARY	13	DIEMAN	HELEN	20
BOAR	ANDREW	9	DODD	JAMES	
BOAR	KATE	INFANT	DRUMMOND	JOHN	24
BOURKE	PATRICK	20	DURCAULT	M	24
BOWDEN	B	20	DURCAULT	LUKE	22
BOYD	ROBERT	25	DURCAULT	ONESSIMA	22
BOYD	TIMOTHY	19	EBERG	FREDERICK	30
BREEN	DANIEL	17	EBERG	ELLEN	25
BROOK	GERARD	20	EBERG	FREDERICK	INFANT
BROOKMAN	JAMES	27	ELLIS	WILLIAM	20
BROOMFIELD	CHARLES	15	FEREY/FERNAY	MARY	24
BROWN	ANN	32	FERGUSON	WILLIAM	29
BROWN	ANN E	22	FETTIS	ALEXANDER	34
BRYANS	EDWARD	23	FETTIS	MARGARET	40
BURKE	MICHAEL	28	FETTIS	MARGARET	4
CAMERA	E S	27	FLANNERY	J	26
CAMPBELL	ROBERT	22	FORGT ?	JOHN	28
CAMPBELL	D	61	FRENCH	W J	22
CAMPBELLISH	J	22	FRENGYNE	P	30
CARMICHAEL	JOSEPH	50	FRESHWELL	DANIEL	37
CARMICHAEL	JOSEPH	20	FRESHWELL	THOMAS	10
CARMICHAEL	ELIZABETH	16	GANLEY	DAVID	20
CARMICHAEL	JESSIE	13	GARBUTT ?	MARTHA	13
CARMICHAEL	DUNCAN	11	GLOUGH	JOHN	
CHASEY	Mr & child		GLOUGH	Mrs	
CHERITON	F	20	GOMRY	JOSEPH	22
CLARK	JOHN	28	GOULBROUGH	JAMES	21
CLARKE	JAMES	22	GOULBROUGH	JOHN	18
CLASEY	JOHN	30	GOULBROUGH	CHARLES	13
CLEMENTS	V C	11	GOURMAN	THOMAS	40
CLEMENTS	WILLIAM	25	GRAY	SAMUEL	28
CLOFIELD	JAMES	30	GRAY	JOHN	26

Passengers and crew unaccounted for and presumed lost.

Surname	Other Names	Age	Surname	Other Names	Age
GREEN	THOMAS	22	JOSEPH	B A	18
GREENMAN	PATRICK	16	JOSEPH	B J	43
GREGORY	JAMES	12	KELLY	ROBERT	20
GRIFFITHS	SARAH	29	KERWIN	ANDREW	21
HARAM	FREDERICK	24	KERWIN	JAMES	24
HARMOOD	JOHN	26	KEWLEY	EDWARD	2nd mate
HARPER	MARY	38	KEYLMACK	W	48
HARPER	JOHN	12	KINGSLEY	WILLIAM	30
HARPER	MARY	9	KLATTENHOFF	HENRY	28
HARPER	MARIA	6	KOPPIA		23
HARPER	WILLIAM	8	LAGO	WILLIAM	50
HARPER	EUPHEMIA	INFANT	LAY	RICHARD	21
HAYES	MRS	28	LAY	SAMUEL	50
HAYES	ELIZA	2	LEAR	EDWARD	19
HELZEL/HOLZEL	AUGUSTA	40	LEGEUET ?	PETER	30
HENDERSON	ISABELLA	30	L'ESTRANGE	ARTHUR	27
HENDERSON	ANDREW	50	L'ESTRANGE	MARY	27
HENDERSON	MRS	45	LETIE	CONDIE	18
HENDERSON	ALEXANDER	12	LEWIS	EDMUND	35
HENDERSON	MARY	11	LINCHEON	WILLIAM	18
HENDERSON	MARGARET	8	LUNT	THOMAS	28
HENDERSON	GEORGE	7	LUNT	ELIZABETH	33
HIGGEN	JAMES	28	LUNT	DAVID	7
HINSTON	THOMAS	26	LYNCH	PATRICK	21
HINSTON	MARY	22	LYSON	JOSEPH	28
HOGG	ELLEN	35	MARBERG	H	30
HOGG	MARION	22	MARBERG	MRS	28
HOLDEN	J	49	MARION/MERION	JAMES	23
HOLLINAX	EDWARD	38	MAYMAN	JOHN	30
HOLT	SARAH E	28	McCOLLOGH	ELIZA	22
HOOD	ANDREW	28	McDONALD	WILLIAM	21
HORST	ANN	28	McGEE	A	35
HOWE	MARK	42	McGILL	MARY	25
HOWELL	HENRY	39	McGRATH	JOHN	36
HOWELL	RICHARD H	9	McGUIRE	C	23
HOWELL	EDWARD	26	McKENZIE	PETER	28
HUGHES	RICHARD	23	McKENZIE	JOHN	48
HUGHES	GEORGE	37	McKENZIE	MARY	46
HUGHES	ELLEN	25	McKENZIE	MATILDA	24
ISAAC	A	28	McKENZIE	MARY	15
JAFFRAY	MR	35	McKENZIE	FANNY	25
JAFFRAY	MRS	35	McKITTOCK	WILLIAM	21
JAFFRAY	WILLIAM	17	McLETCHIE	J	28
JAFFRAY	JESSIE	16	McMICKIN	JOHN	24
JAFFRAY	JOHN	12	McNOUGHTON	P	20
JAFFRAY	GRAHAM	10	McPHERSON	THOMASINA	21
JAFFRAY	MARGARET	8	McPHERSON	AGNES	2
JAFFRAY	CHARLES	2	McPHERSON	JOHN	31
JAFFRAY	ALFRED	2	McVEY	M	17
JAMES	JOHN	40	McWHIRR	JOHN	33
JENKINS	PHIL	23	MIDDLETON	ROBERT	28
JOHNSTON	JAMES	17	MIDDLETON	MRS	26
JONES	SUSAN	24	MILLER	MARGARET	18
JONES	ELIZA	22	MILLER	WILLIAM	11
JONES	JANE	20	MILLER	THOMAS	8
JONES	ELLEN	18	MILLER	ANNE	27
JONES	WILLIAM	24	MILLER	ELLEN	INFANT
JOSEPH	P C	24	MILLER	GILES	37
JOSEPH	P L	20	MILNER	Mr	
JOSEPH	P L C	INFANT	MITCHELL	JANE	50

Passengers and crew unaccounted for and presumed lost.

Surname	Other Names	Age	Surname	Other Names	Age
MITCHELL	JAMES	21	SCOTT	WILLIAM	23
MITCHELL	THOMAS	35	SLELLGAN	D	23
MONTGOMERY	J	28	SLEYERTY	L	33
MOORE	SAMUEL	45	SMITH	MARGARET	38
MOORE	CATHRINE	20	STANLAKE	MARY	62
MOORE	JAMES	INFANT	STANLAKE	SAMUEL	62
MOREN	A	30	STANLAKE	MARY	27
MORAN	CHARLES	26	STANLAKE	SUSAN	19
MORAN	JOHN	24	STOTT	THOMAS	29
MORGAN	JOHN	21	STOTT	SARAH	26
MORGAN	DANIEL	34	SURRI / SURRU	R J	26
MORRISON	ROBERT	12	SUTTON	JOHN	19
MORRISON	ISAAC	25	SUTTON	DANIEL	53
NICHOLL	WILLIAM	25	SUTTON	JANE	23
NICHOLLS	Mr		SWIFT	THOMAS	22
NICHOLSEN	ROBERT DAVID	26	SWIFT	MARY	47
NICHOLSEN	DAVID	21	SWIFT	MARY E	14
O'BRIEN	JULIA	33	SYMONDS	WILLIAM	20
O'CONNOR	JAMES M	22	TALLWELL	EDWARD	21
OLIVER	GEORGE	32	THAIN	PETER	25
OLIVER	BETSY	30	THAIN	MRS	30
OLIVER	CHARLOTTE	11	THAIN	JOHN	INFANT
OLIVER	LOUISA	6	THOMAS	HENRY	38
O'RILEY	M	13/18	TIBBUTT	THOMAS	26
PALMER	MRS	28	TOWN	WILIAM	42
PATTEN	WILLIAM	23	TOWN	JOHN	19
PEARSON	ROBERT	26	TRACY	Y	13
PEARSON	THOMAS	23	WALKER	JAMES	24
PEAT	ANN	22	WALSEY	GEORGE	18
PENLOA	MISS		WARDLAW	JAMES	37
PIEREE / PIERCE	Mr		WARDLAW	C	27
PHAFF	JOSEPH	22	WAYER	F	36
PORTER	JAMES	23	WEBB	H	13/18
POSTLETHWAITE	THOMAS	36	WEBSTER	CATHERINE	34
POSTLETHWAITE	SARAH	32	WHATSON	THOMAS	23
POSTLETHWAITE	THOMAS	8	WHITE	MRS	
POSTLETHWAITE	JANE	6	WHITE	RICHARD	
POSTLETHWAITE	MARTHA	28	WHITE	HONORA	
POSTLETHWAITE	MARTHA	INFANT	WHITTALL	THOMAS	42
PRICE	CHARLES	48	WILD	Elizabeth Ann	20
PYLE	CHARLES	18	WILLIAMS	E H	28
RAINES	BETSY	28	WILLS	ESTHER	27
REAR	THOMAS	33	WILSON	MR	
REGMAN	HENRY	23	WILSON	DAVID M	25
RILEY	SUSAN	33	WILSON	JOHN R	19
RILEY	WILLIAM	33	WILSON	THOMAS	23
ROSE	GEORGE	44	WLSENBACH ?	C	33
ROSE	MRS	43	WORKHOUSE	THOMAS	41
ROSE	BARBARA	16	WRIGHT	DAVID	38
ROSE	JOHN	14	WRIGHT	THOMAS	40
ROSE	GRACE	9			
ROSE	DONALD	7			
ROSE	ANDREW	5			
ROSE	ISABELLA	2			
ROWE	A	43			
RYAN	MICHAEL	30/50			
RYMES	Mrs				
SAMBELLS	FRANCIS	23			
SAMBELLS	MARY	25			
SCHUL	ROBERT	26			

Passenger Survivors.

Surname	Other Names	Ticket	Surname	Other Names	Ticket
INFANT 9 mon.	'Ocean Child'		COPPIN	FRANCIS	2nd class
ABRAHAMSON	H	Steerage	CORMICK	PATRICK	Steerage
ADDISON	WALKER	3rd class	CORMICK/CORMACK	MICHAEL	Steerage
AISLABIE	JOHN	2nd class	COTTRAN	T	2nd class
ALEXANDER	R	2nd class	COWLEY	ALFRED	Intermediate
ANGUS	DAVID	Steerage	COX	JOHN	2nd class
ARENABERG ?	F	2nd class	CRAWFORD	GEORGE	Steerage
ASHBY	THOMAS W	1st class	CROP	THOMAS	Steerage
BADCOCK	W K	Saloon	CROSS	THOMAS	Steerage
BALL	ALEXANDER	Intermediate	CUDDY	WILLIAM	1st class
BAILEY	PATRICK	Steerage	CUTTS	GEORGE	1st class
BARBIER		Intermediate	DAVISON/DAVIDSON	ROBERT	Intermediate
BARR	JOHN	3rd class	DAWSON	ROBERT	Intermediate
BARROW	CHARLES	Steerage	DE COMERA	A	Intermediate
BARTON	W	Steerage	DIAMOND	JOHN	Steerage
BAYARD		Intermediate	DOITE	M	Intermediate
BELL	JOE	Intermediate	DOLTS	M	Intermediate
BENTZ		Steerage	DOWNES	GEORGE	2nd class
BERLETT	J R	1st class	DRISCOLL	D	Steerage
BERR	ALEXANDER	3rd class	DUROW		1st class
BERRYMAN	J	Intermediate	DUROW	A	1st class
BERRYMAN	JAMES	Intermediate	DUROW	M	1st class
BISHOP	SAMUEL	1st class	EDDY	JAMES	2nd class
BISHOP	WILLIAM	1st class	ELLIOTT	SAMUEL	Steerage
BLAIR	W J	Intermediate	FAHY	A	Steerage
BOWDEN	FRANCIS	1st class	FAPH	JOHN	Intermediate
BOWDEN	B	1st class	FINLAY	PETER	Intermediate
BOWDEN	SAMUEL	1st class	FISHER	GEORGE	1st class
BRAYMAN	H	2nd class	FITTESS	ALEXANDER	2nd class
BRIDGEMAN	HENRY	Steerage	FLEMMING	MICHAEL	2nd class
BROCKMAN	S	Intermediate	FOTTRELL	EDWARD	
BROWNE	J	Steerage	FOY	JOHN	Intermediate
BROWNE	RICHARD P	Steerage	FRAMAINE	P F	1st class
BROWNE	THOMAS	Steerage	FRAZER	ALEXANDER	Steerage
BRUGMANN	H	2nd class	FRAZER	HUGH	Steerage
BURKE	GERALD	2nd class	FRIEND	JOHN	3rd class
BURNS	E	Intermediate	GARNETT	GEORGE	Intermediate
BYRNE	MICHAEL	Intermediate	GEFFREY	W	Intermediate
CADDY	WILLIAM	1st class	GIBBEN	RICHARD	Intermediate
CAMERA	A DE	Intermediate	GIBBLE ?	W	2nd class
CARLEY	SAMUEL	Intermediate	GIBSON	JOHN	2nd class
CARLEY	SARAH ANN	Intermediate	GILL	JOE	1st class
CARLEY	ROBERT	Intermediate	GILL	JOHN	Intermediate
CARTER	JONATHAN	3rd class	GOOD	W	Steerage
CARTY	JOHN	3rd class	GORDON	W A	2nd class
CARTY	ANNE	3rd class	GREEN	MICHAEL	Intermediate
CATTRAM	THOMAS	2nd class	GREEN	THOMAS	Steerage
CATTS	G	1st class	GRIMES	G F	1st class
CHASEY	Mrs		GRIMES	ELLEN A	1st class
CHADDICK	C	Steerage	GRUNDY	JOHN	1st class
CHAMBERLAIN	G F	Intermediate	HACKNEY	DAVID	Intermediate
CHERRY	R	Intermediate	HADLEY	SAMUEL	1st class
CLACEY	Mrs REBECCA		HAHR / HAHN	FRED	Intermediate
CLARKE	WILLIAM	1st class	HALL	E	Steerage
COHEN	PATRICK	Steerage	HARPEN	JAMES	Steerage
COLINS	W	Steerage	HARPER	JOHN	Steerage
COLLINS	JOHN	Steerage	HEGARTY	J W	1st class
COMBILLACH	THOMAS	1st class	HERMAN		Intermediate
CONNOR	THOMAS	Steerage	HIGGINS	Mr	
CONSTANTINE	THOMAS	Steerage	HOLLAND	ROBERT	1st class

Passenger Survivors.

Surname	Other Names	Ticket	Surname	Other Names	Ticket
HUNT	MICHAEL	2nd class	RUTHERFORD	Mrs / Miss	
HUNTLEY	STEPHEN	Steerage	RYAN	C	Steerage
HURST	MICHAEL	2nd class	RYDER	RICHARD	Intermediate
JACKSON	ALBERT	2nd class	RYDER	JOHN	Intermediate
JAMES	THOMAS	Intermediate	RYDER	WILLIAM	Intermediate
JENKIN	PHILLIP	3rd class	RYMES	JAMES	2nd class
JENKINS	SAMUEL	Intermediate	RYMES	child	2nd class
JOHNSTON	THOMAS	1st class	SAWDY	WILLIAM	
JOHNSTON	FRANCIS	1st class	SEE	WILLIAM	2nd class
JOHNSTON	JOHN	Steerage	SHAE	F S	2nd class
JONES	W	1st class	SHAWE	JAMES	Intermediate
KEMP	THOMAS	1st class	SHERIDAN	RICHARD	1st class
KERKHOUSE	THOMAS	Intermediate	SHEWELL	R	Steerage
KLATIERSHAFT	B	Steerage	SLOAN	HAMILTON	Intermediate
KOPPIN		3rd class	SMERIL ?	R	3rd class
LAMANE	AUGUST	Intermediate	SMITH	J	2nd class
LANSON/ LANNON	R T	1st class	SPENCER	W	2nd class
LEAHY / LEABY	RICHARD	2nd class	STARMAN	WILLIAM	2nd class
LEE	CHARLES EDWARD	2nd class	STENHARDT	LORENZO	Intermediate
LEGGE ?	WILLIAM	Intermediate	STODHART	JAMES	1st class
LENEHAN	WILLIAM	Steerage	SWAN	JOHN	Steerage
LEWIS	GEORGE	Intermediate	SWIFT	J	Intermediate
LLOYD	THOMAS	Intermediate	TAYLOR	THOMAS	Steerage
LUSCAM	JOHN	2nd class	THOMAS	JOHN	1st class
LYONS	ALEXANDER	Steerage	THOMAS	WILLIAM	3rd class
MAGEE	A	Steerage	THOMAS	SAMUEL	Intermediate
MARIO		Intermediate	THOMAS	A	1st class
MATHEWS	M	3rd class	THOMPSON	JOHN	2nd class
McBRIDE	GEORGE	Steerage	THOMPSON	JAMES	2nd class
McCARLEY	W	Steerage	THOMPSON	WILLIAM	Saloon
McKAY	J	Steerage	THOMPSON	R	Steerage
McKAY	JAMES	Steerage	TIBERTON	THOMAS	1st class
McMAHON	PATRICK	Steerage	TITISS	ALEXANDER	2nd class
McNAUGHTEN	JOHN	1st class	TOBIN	JAMES	Intermediate
MEARA / MEARS	THOMAS	3rd class	TODHUNTER	JOSEPH	2nd class
MILLER	J	2nd class	TOUGH TOY	SAMUEL	1st class
MONTFORD	J	Steerage	TEW	EDWARD	2nd class
MOODY	THOMAS	Steerage	TURNER	W	2nd class
NICHOLLS	JOHN		TWILL	THOMAS	Intermediate
O'BRIEN	JOHN	Steerage	VIVERS	WILLIAM	Intermediate
OLDFIELD	JAMES	Steerage	VIRGOZ		2nd class
ORGAN	JAMES	Steerage	VON-BOURG ?		Intermediate
ORMSBERG	FRANCIS	2nd class	VONT	JOHN	2nd class
OUFFERHT	JOHN	2nd class	WARD	THOMAS	1st class
PERRARD		Intermediate	WATSON	B	2nd class
PHILLIPS	JOHN	2nd class	WATSON	JAMES	
PHILLIPS	W	2nd class	WATSON	JOHN	Steerage
POLE		1st class	WEARNE	RICHARD	1st class
POPHAM	JAMES	Steerage	WEARON	JOSEPH	1st class
PORTER	JOHN		WETYLE	A	1st class
PORTER	WILIAM		WHITMASH	JAMES	Intermediate
POWELL	JOSEPH		WILLET	Mr	
PRATT	E	2nd class	WILLIAMS	JAMES	Intermediate
PRICE	Mr		WILLITE	THOMAS	Steerage
PROCKMAN	STEPHEN	Intermediate	WILSON	J	2nd class
RALEIGH	JAMES	Steerage	WORM	JAMES	Intermediate
REIDY / RIEDY	MICHAEL	2nd class	YATES	GEORGE	Intermediate
RICHMOND	JAMES	Steerage	YEO / YEG	RICHARD	2nd class
RIMES	G T	2nd class			
ROBINSON	J F	1st class			

Crew Survivors.

Surname	Other Names	Sailing as	Surname	Other Names	Sailing as
ACHAN	CHINESE MAN 1	SEAMAN	NOBLE	JOHN	CAPTAIN
ADAMS	M A R	PURSER	PRAIRAM	SIMON	STEWARD
AFFOR	CHINESE MAN 2	SEAMAN	PRATT	E	2ND PURSER
APPOW	CHINESE MAN 3	SEAMAN	RAY	WILLIAM	APPRENTICE
AYLMER	JOHN	SEAMAN	REED	PETER	BOY SEAMAN
BAILEY	PATRICK	SEAMAN	RENDELL	W	ASS. STEWARD
BROWNE	JAMES	SEAMAN	RICE	JOHN	COOK
BURBAN	JOHN	SEAMAN	ROBERTS	JOHN	SEAMAN
BURKE	THOMAS	STEWARD	ROBERTS	THOMAS	SEAMAN
COCK	WILLIAM	PASS. STEWARD	ROBERTS	FJ/TJ?	STEWARD
CONDAIV	NICHOLAS	SEAMAN	ROLANDO	DEMETRI	SEAMAN
COOK	WILLIAM	PASS. STEWARD	ROWLAND	THOMAS	SEAMAN
COWAN	HUGH	3RD OFFICER	SAUNDERSON	JOHN	SEAMAN
COWEN / COWAN	WILLIAM	APPRENTICE	SHEARDEN	W D	SAILMAKER
DENIS	WILLIAM	SEAMAN	SKELLZIG	W	BOATSWAIN
FERGUSON	J	PASS. STEWARD	TAYLOR	W	STEWARD
FITZSIMON	HENRY	SEAMAN	TROTTER	WILLIAM	PASS. COOK
FRAZER	JOHN	CARPENTER	TRUMBELL	THOMAS	PASS. SERVANT
GEORGE	NICHOLAS	SEAMAN	WALLACE	WILLIAM	SEAMAN
GREENAB	JOHN	STEWARD	WEST	HENRY	APPRENTICE
HARPER	THOMAS	STEWARD	WILLIAM / WILLIAMS	JOHN	SEAMAN
HUMPHREY	GEORGE	ASS. PURSER	WILLIS	JOHN	SEAMAN
HUNT	FREDERICK	SEAMAN	WOLECHEWICK	EDWARD	STEWARD
IRVINE	J	SEAMAN		PETER	SEAMAN
JACK	ARCHIBALD	COOKS MATE			
JONES	JOHN	SEAMAN			
JULIAN	JUDGE	SEAMAN			
LEENEHAN	W	COOK			
LENNAN	JOSEPH M	SEAMAN			
LENNON	W	COOK			
MACLEAN	ARCHIBALD	SEAMAN			
MAHIR	JOHN	SEAMAN			
MARTIN	JOHN	SEAMAN			
MAVROMATI	JOHN	SEAMAN			
MAXWELL	JOHN	SEAMAN			
McLELLAN	CHARLES	SEAMAN			
McLELLEN/ MCLALLAN	JOSEPH	SEAMAN			
MITCHELL	JAMES	SEAMAN			
MURPHY	ROSS	SEAMAN			
MURPHY	MICHAEL	CHIEF MATE			
NICHOLAS	ANTONIO	SEAMAN			

On February 4th, two weeks after the loss of the 'Tayleur', the Fife 'Pittenweem Register' reported the fate of seven local people, included the heroic Dr Cunningham, who were passengers aboard the vessel. The newspaper interviewed James Watson, a stonemason, of Cellardyke, Fife, one of the two local survivors. Watson eventually emigrated to Australia where he lived to be 81 years of age. His descendants now number several hundreds.

Even two weeks after the catastrophe the newspaper accounts giving the numbers lost and those saved are hopelessly inaccurate. Although the disaster made national headlines the story quickly faded from press reports because of extensive accounts of the approach and onset of the Crimean War.

'The melancholy details of his dreadful calamity are now told. There were persons belonging to this neighbourhood on board, namely, Dr. R.Hannah, wife and child, Kingsmuir, drowned; David Nicolson, mason, Pittenweem, do; Thomas Wilson, mason, Pittenweem, do; David Pratt, seaman, a native of Cellardyke, but now residing in Dundee, saved; and James Watson, mason, Cellardyke, do., - so that out of this list of seven, only the two last are now living, one of whom, James Watson, gives the following particulars: About 12 o'clock, noon, I was in bed, when David Nicholson came below and said the ship was near land , and that we were in danger; Thomas Wilson was sea-sick, and lay still, but I went on deck immediately, and was there only a short time when she struck on Lambay Island. This might be about one o'clock. A rope was attached to the island from the vessel, and many of the people were getting on shore by it. I resolved to get on shore by that means, if possible, and advised David Nicolson to follow me, but he declined, thinking the vessel I would hold together. It was with difficulty I could get at the rope, from the crowd of passengers which surrounded that part of the vessel to which it was attached, but I at length succeeded, and warped myself on shore. Scarcely had I reached the Island, when the ship gave a lurch which broke the rope, and all on it were cast into the sea and drowned. After I was on the island, I saw David Nicolson standing on the deck, and called and beckoned on him to come; but I never saw Thomas Wilson, which might be cased by the number of people on deck. David Nicolson, was 21 years of age, and Thomas Wilson, 23. (The number on board, including crew, was 374, - out of this number 344 drowned, and 30 saved. A Coroners Inquest is investigating the cause which led to this direful calamity.'

INDEX

THETIS

"The Admiralty Regrets..."

The disaster in Liverpool Bay

C. Warren & J. Benson

Thetis - the Admiralty Regrets. The disaster in Liverpool Bay. A minute by minute account of the submarine disaster that cost the lives of 99 men...... Why didn't anyone cut open the submarine? Why was there no urgency in the Admiralty's rescue system? Did the Admiralty **really** regret?
Contains previously unpublished photographs and documents.
By C. Warren & J. Benson. Foreword by Derek Arnold, a survivor's son, and postscript by maritime historian David Roberts.
ISBN 1 9521020 8 0. £9.50.

The sinking of the Thetis costs 99 men their lives and is still today the worst submarine disaster in British History. The book contains interviews with relatives of victims; sons, daughters, brothers, sisters and those very rare ladies, living widows.

Also here are never before seen documents from the time; Offers of outside help, secret Navy reports and even descriptions of bodies for identification.

Why did the Official Inquiry blame nobody, explaining it away as 'an unfortunate sequence of events'?

Why did civil action on behalf of the widows fail?

Why did the Admiralty cover it up?

How much did Churchill know?

How were those left behind treated?

A huge publicly subscribed disaster fund was collected for the relatives.

How was this managed and distributed? Who got what and why? What ever happened to the money that was left?

'Secrets and Scandals' is a shocking revelation of the establishment, all the way up to Churchill, closing ranks whilst the 'lower orders' were treated in a manner that was simply unforgivable.

HMS THETIS - Secrets and Scandal
Aftermath of a Disaster
By David Roberts
ISBN: 0 9521020 0 5

Lusitania - On the 7th May 1915 the Cunard vessel *Lusitania* was torpedoed by a German submarine off the Old Head of Kinsale on the south west coast of Ireland, resulting in the loss of the vessel itself and 1,201 men, women, and children. An act of brutal aggression? Or a cynical plot to bring the United States into the First World War?

More than eighty years on the story of the *Lusitania* continues to be shrouded in mystery and suspicion. What was her real cargo? Why wasn't she protected? Why did she sink so quickly?

Lord Mersey, the great grandson of the man who chaired the enquiry into the *Lusitania* disaster, (who he calls 'the Old Man'), has been extremely helpful and was kind enough to write a new foreword for this Special Edition.

Containing rare photographs from Germany and elsewhere, it is a truly intriguing and fascinating tale.

'A book that clamours to be read' - Observer.

'The truth at last' - The Sunday Times.

By Colin Simpson. ISBN 1 9521020 6 4. £9.50.

Other Books available from Avid

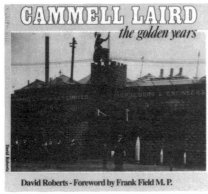

Cammell Laird - the golden years
'Captures life in the prosperous years
of the historic shipyard'. -
Liverpool Echo
ISBN: 1 9521020 2 1 £5.99

**Faster Than The Wind - The Liverpool
to Holyhead Telegraph**
by Frank Large

ISBN: 1 9521020 9 9 £8.95

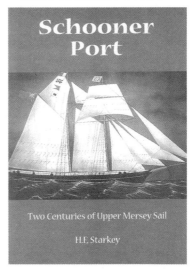

Life at Lairds
Memories of working shipyard men
at Cammell Lairds world famous
shipyard.
ISBN: 0 9521020 1 3 £6.99

**Schooner Port - Two Centuries of Upper
Mersey Sail** by H.F. Starkey
'Recognised as the only authoritative
work on this particlur subject'. - *Sea
Breezes*
ISBN: 0 9521020 4 6 £8.95

Videos

Cammell Laird, Old Ships and Hardships - the history and true story of this world-famous shipyard - on video. Contains rare archive footage of famous vessels and comments from the men who built them. £12.99.

All In A Day's Work Vol. 1 - the story of a living, working river - the River Mersey - and the ordinary people that work upon it. Features : Mersey Pilots; Pilot Launch Crews; Shipbuilding and Shiprepairing workers; Dredger crews, and much more. £12.99

All In A Day's Work Vol 2 - More stories from the Mersey, on video. Features : Rock Boats; Mersey Ferries; Tugs and Tug management; the Bunker boats and crews; the Vessel Tracking System; New vessels on the river including cruise liners and car ferries, & much more. £12.99